INSTRUCTOR'S MANUAL

■ THE ■
SUCCESSFUL
MARKETING
■ PLAN ■

SECOND EDITION

THE SUCCESSFUL MARKETING PLAN

SECOND EDITION

A Disciplined and Comprehensive Approach

ROMAN G. HIEBING, JR.
SCOTT W. COOPER

NTC Business Books
a division of NTC/Contemporary Publishing Company
Lincolnwood, Illinois USA

CONTENTS

OVERVIEW

The purpose of the Instructor's Manual is two-fold:

1. Assist the instructor's use of *The Successful Marketing Plan* as a teaching tool.

2. Share the authors' experiences in the planning and teaching and in the application of promotional and advertising campaigns courses.

Prior to publication of the first edition, *The Successful Marketing Plan* had been used as the basic text in manuscript form for promotional campaigns with both Journalism and Business students over a two-year period. After each session, the text was rewritten, based on input from the students and the authors' direct classroom experience. Since its original publication in 1990, the text has been adopted by a cross-section of colleges and universities. It has been used extensively in marketing management and marketing communications courses, as well as campaigns, survey of marketing, and marketing planning programs. It has also been used as a supplement to marketing research courses. The second edition of *The Successful Marketing Plan* has been revised and expanded, based on use of the first edition by faculty and students over the past five years.

The text makes a very pragmatic, real-world approach to preparing a marketing plan for consumer goods producers, business to business firms, and service or retail organizations. The basics taught are being used every day by marketing and advertising practitioners, thus giving students an opportunity to realistically apply in the classroom the methods used in the business world.

The text applies an easy-to-teach and easy-to-understand, step-by-step methodology. It achieves results if the students can be continually motivated to both read and apply, on a timely basis, the principles and examples set forth in the book as the course unfolds.

The authors believe you will find *The Successful Marketing Plan* , 2nd ed., the one definitive source for your classroom. It provides a comprehensive and disciplined approach that brings together previous marketing and communications courses taken by students into a workable and unified marketing plan that is used as the foundation for the actual advertising campaign. It is our hope that this guide will not only help provide a stimulating class atmosphere but, just as important, assist your students in entering the world of advertising and marketing as emerging practitioners.

The Instructor's Manual is divided into three major sections. The first section provides *suggestions for utilizing the text* in the teaching of an applications course, such as promotional campaigns, or a more traditional marketing management or marketing communications course. The second section provides *exam questions* and a *case test* that can also be employed as a background piece for a class project in either an "applications" or traditional lecture course. And the third section discusses the *organizational elements* of an applications campaigns course.

TEXT APPLICATION

The instructor's manual was designed to provide instructional assistance for using *The Successful Marketing Plan* as a classroom tool. Section 1 will give you a chapter-by-chapter review of the text, with tips and ideas for lectures and class discussions. Section 2 offers example test questions and a case study. Section 3 provides suggestions for structuring and teaching an applications-oriented "Campaigns" course.

The objectives for this section of the manual are as follows:

— Highlight the key areas of each chapter to be reviewed by the instructor with students.

— Provide assistance to the instructor with those specific elements of each chapter that students have questions and/or difficulty understanding.

— Provide exercises, when necessary, that the instructor can use with the students to help them grasp the meaning of specific ideas within each chapter. However, because the text is relatively easy to understand due to its step-by-step "how to" structure, this section of the manual is designed to help the instructor do less pure lecturing and more interacting with students by discussing, challenging, and providing assistance to students in application of methods and principles.

Ideally, if the instructor has the time, it would be best to read through the text and then through the manual, tailoring the teaching structure provided in each chapter of this guide to the specific course objectives. Then, review the discussion of each chapter in the manual just prior to its presentation in class in order to be prepared for the class lecture and students' questions.

Chapter Objectives

1. Define the following:

   — marketing

   — marketing plan

   — disciplined marketing planning

2. Discuss the process, steps, and elements of disciplined marketing planning.

3. Discuss how to use the disciplined approach in developing an effective marketing plan.

Teaching Suggestions

1. First define *marketing*: the process of determining the target market for your product or service, detailing the target market's needs and wants and fulfilling these needs and wants better than the competition. Then define *marketing plan*: an arranged structure designed to guide the process of determining the target market, its needs and wants and fulfilling these needs and wants better than the competition. Finally, explain that *disciplined marketing planning* is the particular method used to facilitate the process of target market determination and fulfillment of the target's needs. Stress that the marketing planning process is *not a solution* in and of itself but a methodology which will ensure development of solutions. It is important for students to realize this is not a case study course. They will not be studying old solutions and applying them to new problems. Rather, they will be encouraged to utilize the disciplined development methodology to evolve their own solutions—solutions rooted in the reality of the target market's needs and the inherent attributes of the product relative to the competitive environment.

2. Make sure it is made clear that disciplined planning means following an ordered, interlocking, step-by-step method, rather than jumping ahead or indiscriminately preparing just one portion of the plan. It means having adequate information in hand and making the necessary decisions to prepare each portion of the marketing plan. For example, unless there is a very thorough understanding and succinct determination of the target market, the marketing positioning will not be accurate. The marketing planning process involves four major components:

   — Marketing background

   — Marketing plan

   — Marketing execution

   — Marketing evaluation

   All four components are important, and each step in the process must be rigorously followed.

There must first be a base of information (the marketing background) before a workable plan can be built to meet sales expectations (refer to the Disciplined Marketing Planning chart on the next page). Next, a company's product sales are generated from the target market. With the right target market determination, appropriate marketing objectives can be set and plan strategies described that will affect the behavior of the target market so the sales goals can be met. Preparing these segments of the marketing plan will provide the insight for developing the communications goals and how an image is to be delivered/communicated via the tactical marketing mix tools such as product, brand pricing, and advertising. Each step in the discipline process interlocks and is dependent upon the previous step. Just as the positioning assists in developing the communication goals, it also provide a direction for the use of the marketing mix tools that follow in the marketing plan.

3. Make an overhead transparency of the chart on the next page and explain what goes into developing the marketing background section and marketing plan section. Walk through each of the ten steps of the marketing planning process, from the business review to the final evaluation and research and testing. Further explain that the execution segment of disciplined marketing planning is the tangible action in the marketplace, such as when a commercial is run or coupon is dropped. Finally, the evaluation step is the determination of whether the objectives throughout the plan were met and the overall plan itself was successful.

4. After reviewing the elements of the disciplined marketing planning process, distribute a blank copy of the chart and have each student in the second day of class fill it in (with their books closed). The better students understand what is involved in disciplined planning, the better they will prepare and organize the marketing background and plan sections as the course unfolds.

5. Another learning exercise is to have each student define the elements on the planning chart. Each element should be defined with different students providing the definitions along with examples of how companies have utilized each market mix tool. The instructor should briefly review some of the idea starters under each marketing mix tool in the "Idea Starters Grid" in Appendix A of the text. These examples can be further explored by the 11 marketing situations delineated in the same Appendix.

6. If the course is applications/cases type in orientation, make it clear that each student will become involved in the planning process, particularly in preparing the background section. While helping to prepare the background section, they should jot down their ideas for the marketing plan and consider them later for the appropriate sections of the plan.

7. Point out that the marketing planning process is very time consuming and, therefore, they should start immediately on the marketing background section with each student making a major contribution early and continually throughout the overall effort.

8. Use the business review worksheets provided in Appendix B of the text to help students understand what information is needed, and how it can be gathered and presented. This will be helpful whether the course is an applications course or a traditional lecture-style class, where the worksheets can be used to discuss examples and cases.

Disciplined Marketing Planning

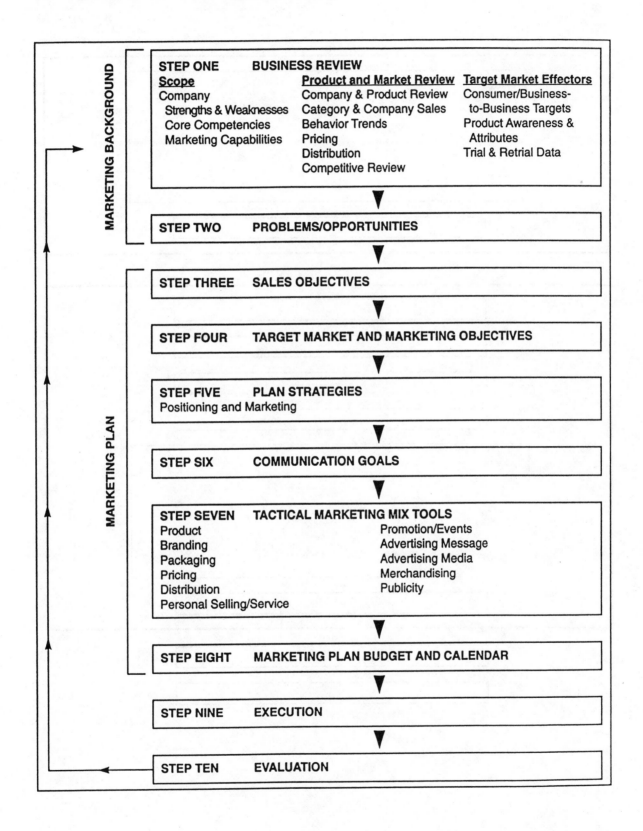

MARKETING BACKGROUND

STEP ONE   BUSINESS REVIEW

<u>Scope</u>	<u>Product and Market Review</u>	<u>Target Market Effectors</u>
Company	Company & Product Review	Consumer/Business-
Strengths & Weaknesses	Category & Company Sales	to-Business Targets
Core Competencies	Behavior Trends	Product Awareness &
Marketing Capabilities	Pricing	Attributes
	Distribution	Trial & Retrial Data
	Competitive Review	

STEP TWO   PROBLEMS/OPPORTUNITIES

MARKETING PLAN

STEP THREE   SALES OBJECTIVES

STEP FOUR   TARGET MARKET AND MARKETING OBJECTIVES

STEP FIVE   PLAN STRATEGIES
Positioning and Marketing

STEP SIX   COMMUNICATION GOALS

STEP SEVEN   TACTICAL MARKETING MIX TOOLS

Product	Promotion/Events
Branding	Advertising Message
Packaging	Advertising Media
Pricing	Merchandising
Distribution	Publicity
Personal Selling/Service	

STEP EIGHT   MARKETING PLAN BUDGET AND CALENDAR

STEP NINE   EXECUTION

STEP TEN   EVALUATION

Disciplined Marketing Planning

8. It should also be pointed out on a regular basis that although the planning process should be very disciplined and orderly, there will be continuous revisions of the plan as new data is discovered and the many segments of the plan are interfaced. For example, after the advertising strategy is written and ads are being developed, it might be discovered sales goals cannot be met unless there is a promotion advertising strategy as well. Or, the media plan calling for the use of four mediums must be reduced to three because the overall marketing budget cannot profitably generate the required sales. Accordingly, it seems the final marketing budget and calendar are continually being revised until the final campaign report is submitted.

9. Emphasize the fact that the marketing planning process presented in the text is a general framework which must be adjusted and adapted to the specific situation. It may vary according to the firm or industry to which it is applied, the nature and extent of information available, parameters defined by management, whether the product is new or mature, or any number of other variables. Some sections may receive more emphasis, and others less or may even be left out of a plan entirely if it does not apply. This is especially important for students of an applications-style course.

Class Discussion/Questions

1. What is marketing?

2. What is the difference between marketing versus advertising, promotion, and public relations?

3. What is a marketing plan?

4. What is disciplined marketing planning?

5. What is the difference between planning and execution?

6. Why is a product's chance for success dramatically reduced when the marketer executes before planning? For example, a marketer runs an ad featuring low price when in fact the target market makes their purchase decision primarily on quality. This is an all-too-typical situation where the marketer did not thoroughly define the target needs and wants before preparing the advertising execution.

7. In the Disciplined Marketing Planning process which takes longer to complete, the Marketing Background or the Marketing Plan segment? Why?

8. Discuss the importance of understanding marketing planning. For example, without thoroughly understanding the product, target market, competition, and positioning, a company could not create an ad which meaningfully communicates the benefits of product versus the competition. Thus it would be difficult to convey the correct image and motivate the consumer to purchase the product.

CHAPTER 1

THE BUSINESS REVIEW

Chapter Objectives

1. Define the following:

   — Industry category

   — Consumers

   — Customers

   — Business Review

   — SIC

   — Primary Research

   — Quantitative Research

   — Qualitative Research

   — Secondary Research

2. Provide students with an overview of the business review process.

3. Help students learn the components of a business review.

4. Have students prepare a business review outline for a consumer, business to business, or retail and/or service organization.

5. Provide an overview as to the types of research necessary for compiling a business review.

6. Teach students how to use indexing as a way to present a number, or group of numbers, in relation to an average, or base number.

7. Discuss sources of information that can be used to compile a business review.

Teaching Suggestions

1. Primary Elements of a Business Review: Review the individual steps of a business review provided in pages 8–11. Discuss the purpose of each, and where one might gather information for each. It is helpful to have a basic understanding of the business review structure before beginning to apply it to a particular business.

2. Outline, p. 7: Choose a business you are familiar with and discuss what you would need to know about that business before completing a business review. Use the questions after each of the ten major steps in Chapter 2 as a guide to the types of information you would need. This should be kept in the context of an overview intended to give students a broad feel for the types of

information that are needed. Based on this particular case, develop an outline similar to the generic one provided on pages 11 to 14. Work with students to determine how the outline should adapt to this case.

3. <u>Suggestions 2-6, pp. 14–17:</u> In preparation for developing a business review, discuss tasks 2-6 in this chapter.

— **Task 2, Develop Questions:** Have students actually list questions for each section of the business review. Format questions can be found after each major topical section in Chapter 2.

— **Task 3, Develop Data Charts:** Have students develop blank data charts intended to capture the information needed to answer the questions. The charts force students to determine ahead of time the information they need to acquire. The charts also help to reduce students' tendencies of simply reporting what was convenient to find at the library.

— **Task 4, Develop Reference Points for Comparison:** Stress the need to develop charts that have reference points for comparison. For example, if students provide sales growth for a category of the company (women's shoes), have them compare that growth against the total average company growth or women's shoe sales nationally. Students should not report facts, but <u>relationships</u>. Relationships or comparisons are the heart of a business review. You don't know if something is good or bad until you compare it to a standard. Here's an example you can use in class to make this point: If company X sales increased 5% last year, is that good or bad?

  – Suppose we knew that sales in each of the last five years increased an average of 15% per year?

  – Suppose we knew that the market, as a whole, increased 10% last year.

With these additional reference points we now know that company X sales growth has slowed and the company is losing market share.

— **Task 5, Conduct Data Search:** Have student teams conduct a data search against a specific company or case (see Section 3 of this manual for case example). Have them utilize the sources of information section starting on page 20 of the text. Also, have students compile a list of sources not found in this book. Then at the end of class have them share those sources with each other. A major benefit of this type of activity is that it teaches students how to find information on their own. Students become users of the information they find, not regurgitaters of information you give them. If the course has an application/case orientation, the more information they find, the better their end product. Below are some additional tips that students might use.

  * Use <u>Standard Rate and Data Service</u> to make a list of all the trade and/or consumer magazines associated with the chosen business. Refer to the magazines for information. Call the magazines to find out if their research department has any studies containing information that will help the group answer questions for any of the business review outline sections.

  Call businesses in the category and see if they will let the groups visit for an interview. It is surprising how many businesses will cooperate.

  Contact a trade association. They will often provide industry data free of charge.

  Conduct an informal research study on users and nonusers of the product. Ask consumers questions at the point-of-purchase. Talk to the trade—a grocer, the manager of a distributorship, etc.

— **Step 6, Write Summary Statements:** Page 105 provides examples of summary statements you can use to demonstrate how this information is to be presented. The key to preparing the business review document is to present the information, including interpretations of tables and charts, in concise, factual statements.

4. <u>Conducting Research, pp. 17–19:</u> Briefly discuss the differences between primary and secondary research as presented in the text. If the class is an applications course, the focus should be on utilizing secondary research. If this class has an application/case study orientation and the students have had a previous primary research class, they could conduct their own research. However, we have found that there is usually more than enough information if the secondary sources are utilized properly. If the text is being used for an application, campaigns or case class and the groups do decide to conduct their own research, samples of a primary research questionnaire for a retailer, a consumer products company, and a service company follow this chapter in the guide. Primary research tends to be used most commonly in measuring awareness, attitudes, attribute preference, and competitive performance ratings on those attributes. On occasion, basic awareness and competitive performance data can be found in trade publications or trade association documents.

5. <u>Indexing, p. 19:</u> Below is an indexing example you can utilize to further demonstrate how indexing can be used to extract information for a business review.

Year	National Category Data Sales	Company X Sales	Index
1992	+10	+10	100
1993	+5	+10	200*
1994	+3	+9	300
1995	+5	+4	80
1996	+5	+3	60

* The index is achieved by dividing company X sales growth by the base or the national category sales growth and multiplying by 100 (10 divided by 5 times 100 = 200).

Results

Company X performed directionally above the category (+10 points or more above the norm or expected value of 100) for the 1992 to '94 period. After that Company X has performed below the category (10 points below the expected norm of 100) for the period of 1995 to 1996. Thus Company X was gaining market share during the first three years and losing market share during the last two years.

Class Discussion/Questions

1. Discuss the importance of consumer information and insight in marketing decision making.

2. Discuss Lauterborn's "Four Cs." Compare and contrast with Kotler's "Four Ps."

3. Why is there a need for a business review?

4. What is the role of questions and data charts in a business review?

5. Why are reference points of comparison necessary when developing a business review?

6. What are the differences between primary and secondary data?

7. Why should business review summary statements be objective in nature?

8. Provide examples of when indexing can be used to show relationships between two sets of data in a business review.

Retail Telephone Questionnaire Example

Shoe Store Chain

INTERVIEWER: _____

NAME: _____

TELEPHONE #: _____

ADDRESS: _____

DATE: _____

START TIME: _____

FINISH TIME: _____

Hello, I'm calling long distance for _____located in _____. We are conducting a survey in the area on shopping for shoes. **(ASK:** Are you the female/male head of the household?) **(DO NOT PAUSE)**

1. Please tell me the name of all stores in the MADISON area where you can purchase shoes or other footwear. **(NOTE THE FIRST RESPONSE IN COLUMN 1-AA; ALL OTHER RESPONSES IN COLUMN 1-A.)** What other stores come to mind?

2. Now let's consider the stores you like to shop at for four types of shoes.

    A. When you need <u>dress</u> shoes for yourself for career and social activities, at which stores do you normally shop? **(RECORD ALL RESPONSES IN COLUMN 2-A)**

    B. When you need comfortable <u>non-athletic casual</u> shoes for yourself for leisure time activities, at which stores do you normally shop? **(RECORD ALL RESPONSES IN COLUMN 2-B)**

    C. When you need everyday all-around <u>leisure time athletic</u> shoes for yourself such as walking shoes, hiking boots, sport sandals, etc., at which stores do you normally shop? **(RECORD ALL RESPONSES IN COLUMN 2-C)**

    D. And when you need <u>high-performance athletic</u> shoes for yourself such as basketball, running, court shoes, etc., at which stores do you normally shop? **(RECORD ALL RESPONSES IN COLUMN 2-D)**

    E. Do you purchase shoes for children under 13 years of age?　　(07)
        1... YES --> At which stores do you normally shop for these children shoes? **(RECORD IN COLUMN 2-E)**
        2... NO --> **GO TO Q3**

3. What is the name of the last store in which you bought any type of shoe? **(ALLOW ONLY ONE RESPONSE -- RECORD IN COLUMN 3)**

4. At what other stores have you purchased shoes in the past year? **(RECORD ALL RESPONSES IN COLUMN 4)**

MADISON

	AWARENESS		NORMALLY SHOP				PURCHASE		
	FIRST Q1-AA	OTHER Q1-A	DRESS Q2-A	CASUAL Q2-B	ATHL LEISURE Q2-C	PERFORM. ATHL Q2-D	CHILD Q2-E	LAST Q3	OTHER Q4
0012 Athletes Foot............	____	____	____	____	____	____	____	____	____
5103 Boot Barn	____	____	____	____	____	____	____	____	____
0501 Boston Store	____	____	____	____	____	____	____	____	____
1354 Cobbies	____	____	____	____	____	____	____	____	____
0601 Cornblooms	____	____	____	____	____	____	____	____	____
0541 Dunhams	____	____	____	____	____	____	____	____	____
1615 Endicott Johnson ...	____	____	____	____	____	____	____	____	____
0001 Famous Footwear.....	____	____	____	____	____	____	____	____	____
0010 Florsheim................	____	____	____	____	____	____	____	____	____
0013 Foot Locker..............	____	____	____	____	____	____	____	____	____
0505 Goldies	____	____	____	____	____	____	____	____	____
0032 Gussini	____	____	____	____	____	____	____	____	____
0031 Hermans	____	____	____	____	____	____	____	____	____
0604 Jack's Shoes	____	____	____	____	____	____	____	____	____
0006 K-Mart.....................	____	____	____	____	____	____	____	____	____
0002 Kinney's...................	____	____	____	____	____	____	____	____	____
0507 Kohl's	____	____	____	____	____	____	____	____	____
0508 Marshall Fields	____	____	____	____	____	____	____	____	____
0614 Morgans/Youthful ..	____	____	____	____	____	____	____	____	____
0605 Movin' Shoes	____	____	____	____	____	____	____	____	____
0606 Monona Bootery	____	____	____	____	____	____	____	____	____
0009 Naturalizer	____	____	____	____	____	____	____	____	____
0008 Payless.....................	____	____	____	____	____	____	____	____	____
0004 J.C.Penney...............	____	____	____	____	____	____	____	____	____
0610 Ragetz	____	____	____	____	____	____	____	____	____
0027 Red Cross	____	____	____	____	____	____	____	____	____
0005 Sears.........................	____	____	____	____	____	____	____	____	____
0623 Shoe Box	____	____	____	____	____	____	____	____	____
0611 Shopko	____	____	____	____	____	____	____	____	____
0003 Thom McAn..............	____	____	____	____	____	____	____	____	____
0016 T.J Maxx	____	____	____	____	____	____	____	____	____
5519 Wal-Mart..................	____	____	____	____	____	____	____	____	____
8812 Younker's	____	____	____	____	____	____	____	____	____

ALL OTHER (WRITE IN BELOW)

_____ ____ ____ ____ ____ ____ ____ ____ ____

_____ ____ ____ ____ ____ ____ ____ ____ ____

_____ ____ ____ ____ ____ ____ ____ ____ ____

_____ ____ ____ ____ ____ ____ ____ ____ ____

NONE ____ ____ ____ ____ ____ ____ ____ ____

MADISON

5A. In thinking about shopping for shoes for yourself, I am going to ask you some questions about six stores that sell footwear. The six stores are **Wal-Mart, Kohls, Boston Store, Famous Footwear, Penneys,** and **Payless.** It is not necessary for you to have shopped in these stores, we are interested only in your opinions.

Considering these six stores **(REPEAT LIST OF STORES)**, which <u>two</u> do you think carry the most fashionable **dress** shoes? When I refer to dress shoes in this question, I mean dress shoes you need for career and social activities. **(INDICATE BELOW WITH A "1" BY MOST FASHIONABLE DRESS)**

	WAL-MART	KOHLS	BOSTON STORE	FAMOUS FOOTWEAR	PENNEYS	PAYLESS
MOST FASHIONABLE DRESS SHOES	(08)	(09)	(10)	(11)	(12)	(13)

Now, only thinking about these six stores **(REPEAT STORES NAMES)**, as I read each of the following items, please tell me which **two** stores you think best meet each item. **REPEAT DESCRIPTION OF SHOE CATEGORY AS NECESSARY.**

	WAL-MART	KOHLS	BOSTON STORE	FAMOUS FOOTWEAR	PENNEYS	PAYLESS
LOWEST PRICES ON DRESS SHOES	(14)	(15)	(16)	(17)	(18)	(19)
BEST SELECTION OF DRESS SHOE **STYLES**	(20)	(21)	(22)	(23)	(24)	(25)
BEST QUALITY DRESS SHOES	(26)	(27)	(28)	(29)	(30)	(31)
BEST SELECTION OF DRESS SHOE **SIZES**	(32)	(33)	(34)	(35)	(36)	(37)
BEST VALUE FOR YOUR MONEY ON DRESS SHOES	(38)	(39)	(40)	(41)	(42)	(43)
HAS THE BEST BRAND NAMES ON DRESS SHOES	(44)	(45)	(46)	(47)	(48)	(49)
HAS THE MOST KNOWLEDGEABLE SALESPEOPLE ABOUT DRESS SHOES	(50)	(51)	(52)	(53)	(54)	(55)
HAS THE BEST SELECTION OF DRESS SHOES **FOR THE WHOLE FAMILY**	(56)	(57)	(58)	(59)	(60)	(61)

5B. Now, thinking about athletic shoes. When I refer to athletic shoes in this question, I mean athletic shoes you need for everyday all-around leisure time or high-performance athletic activities. The six stores we would like to consider for this question are **Wal-Mart, Kohls, Boston Store, Famous Footwear, Foot Locker,** and **Penneys.** It is not necessary for you to have shopped in these stores, we are interested only in your opinions.

Considering these six stores **(REPEAT LIST OF STORES)**, which <u>two</u> do you think carry the most fashionable **athletic** shoes? **(INDICATE BELOW WITH A "1" BY MOST FASHIONABLE ATHLETIC)**

	WAL-MART	KOHLS	BOSTON STORE	FAMOUS FOOTWEAR	FOOT LOCKER	PENNEYS
MOST FASHIONABLE ATHLETIC SHOES						
	(62)	(63)	(64)	(65)	(66)	(67)

Now, only thinking about these same six stores **(REPEAT STORE NAMES)**, as I read each of the following items, please tell me which **two** stores you think best meet each item. **REPEAT DESCRIPTION OF SHOE CATEGORY AS NECESSARY.**

	WAL-MART	KOHLS	BOSTON STORE	FAMOUS FOOTWEAR	FOOT LOCKER	PENNEYS
LOWEST PRICES ON ATHLETIC SHOES						
	(68)	(69)	(70)	(71)	(72)	(73)
BEST SELECTION OF ATHLETIC SHOE **STYLES**						
	(74)	(75)	(76)	(77)	(78)	(79)
				2	* *	* *
				(01) (02)	(03) (04)	(05) (06)
BEST QUALITY ATHLETIC SHOES						
	(07)	(08)	(09)	(10)	(11)	(12)
BEST SELECTION OF ATHLETIC SHOE **SIZES**						
	(13)	(14)	(15)	(16)	(17)	(18)
BEST VALUE FOR YOUR MONEY ON ATHLETIC SHOES						
	(19)	(20)	(21)	(22)	(23)	(24)
HAS THE BEST BRAND NAMES ON ATHLETIC SHOES						
	(25)	(26)	(27)	(28)	(29)	(30)
HAS THE MOST KNOWLEDGEABLE SALESPEOPLE ABOUT ATHLETIC SHOES						
	(31)	(32)	(33)	(34)	(35)	(36)
HAS THE BEST SELECTION OF ATHLETIC SHOES **FOR THE WHOLE FAMILY**						
	(37)	(38)	(39)	(40)	(41)	(42)

NOTE: ASK QUESTION 6 ONLY IF RESPONDENT INDICATED THAT THEY SHOP FOR CHILDREN SHOES IN QUESTION 2E.

6a. Now, thinking about all shoe stores or shoe departments in the area, which <u>two</u> do you think   have the best prices on shoes for children under 13? **WRITE IN STORE NAMES BELOW.**

   Best Prices on Children Shoes:

   _____ (43-46) _____ (47-50)

b. Which <u>two</u> stores do you think have the best selection on shoes for children under 13?   **WRITE IN STORE NAMES BELOW.**

   Best Selection on Children Shoes:

   _____ (51-54) _____ (55-58)

c. Which <u>two</u> stores do you think have the best overall value for your money on shoes for   children under 13? **WRITE IN STORE NAMES BELOW.**

   Best Value on Children Shoes:

   _____ (59-62) _____ (63-66)

d. And which <u>two</u> stores do you think have the best customer service on shoes for   children under 13? **WRITE IN STORE NAMES BELOW.**

   $\underline{3}$ * * * * *
   (01) (02) (03) (04) (05) (06)

   Best Customer Service on Children Shoes:

   _____ (07-10) _____ (11-14)

7-1. Do you participate in any frequent buyer programs or preferred customer programs for <u>any</u> kind of product, service or store?
   (15)
   1 ...   Yes   Which frequent buyer or preferred customer programs do you participate in?

   _____ (16-18) _____ (19-21)

   2 ...   No

   _____ (22-24) _____ (25-27)

   a. What, if anything, do you <u>like</u> about frequent buyer/preferred customer programs?

   _____ (28-29)

   _____ (30-31)

   b. What, if anything, do you <u>not</u> like about frequent buyer/preferred customer programs?

   _____ (32-33)

   _____ (34-35)

7-2. Suppose you were thinking about shopping for shoes and you were deciding between two stores that had the same selection and prices. Which one of the following items would get you to go to one store over the other. **(READ LIST -- ROTATE STARTING POINT)**

   Which of the remaining items **(READ REMAINING ITEMS)** would be next most likely to get you to go to that store?

   CONTINUE WITH REMAINING ITEMS SUCH THAT YOU HAVE RANKED THEM FROM 1 TO 5.

   (36) The store which has an area for children to play
   (37) The store which has video demonstrations on shoe design and use
   (38) The store which has a frequent buyer program
   (39) The store which has knowledgeable salespeople about shoes
   (40) The store which also sell items such as clothes, jewelry, linens, etc.

8. Have you seen or heard any advertising for Famous Footwear in the past three months, that would be since August?

    1 ...Yes ⇒ **ASK 8-1**   **(41)**
    2 ...No ⇒ **GO TO 8-2**

    1. Which of the following types of advertising have you seen or heard for Famous Footwear in the past three months (**READ LIST - CHECK ALL THAT APPLY**).

        (42) Advertising in Sunday newspaper inserts or supplements
        (43) Advertising in the main body of the newspaper
        (44) Television advertising
        (45) Radio advertising
        (46) Billboards
        (47) Received a flier in the mail

    2. Thinking about Famous Footwear, what would be the <u>three</u> leading brand names of shoes you think you would find at Famous Footwear?

        _____   _____   _____
        (48-50)   (51-53)   (54-56)

    a. Have you ever been in a Famous Footwear store?

        1... Yes   **(57)**
        2... No --> **GO TO QUESTION 9**

    b. In the past year, about how many times have you been in a Famous Footwear store? (**PROBE FOR ACTUAL NUMBER OF TIMES**)

        _____TIME(S) **IF NONE -- GO TO QUESTION 9**   (58-59)

    c. On how many of those visits to Famous Footwear in the past year did you actually purchase shoes? (**PROBE FOR ACTUAL NUMBER OF TIMES**)

        _____TIME(S) (**MUST BE LESS THAN OR EQUAL TO Q8b**)   (60-61)

9. Have you seen or heard any <u>**shoe**</u> advertising for Boston Store in the past three months, that would be since August?

    1 ...Yes ⇒ **ASK 9-1**   **(62)**
    2 ...No ⇒ **GO TO 9-2**

    1. Which of the following types of shoe advertising have you seen or heard for Boston Store in the past three months (**READ LIST - CHECK ALL THAT APPLY**).

        (63) Advertising in Sunday newspaper inserts or supplements
        (64) Advertising in the main body of the newspaper
        (65) Television advertising
        (66) Radio advertising
        (67) Billboards
        (68) Received a flier in the mail

    2. Thinking about the Boston Store, what would be the <u>three</u> leading brand names of shoes you think you would find at the Boston Store?

        _____   _____   _____
        (69-71)   (72-74)   (75-77)

    a. In the past year, about how many times have you been in a Boston Store's shoe department? (**PROBE FOR ACTUAL NUMBER OF TIMES**)

        _____TIME(S) **IF NONE -- GO TO QUESTION 10**   (78-79)

        4 *   *   *   *   *
        (01) (02) (03) (04) (05) (06)

16

b. On how many of those visits to Boston Store's shoe department in the past year did you actually purchase shoes? **(PROBE FOR ACTUAL NUMBER OF TIMES)**

_____TIME(S) **(MUST BE LESS THAN OR EQUAL TO Q9a)**   (60-61)

10. Have you seen or heard any **shoe** advertising for Kohls in the past three months, that would be since August?

    1 ...Yes ⇒ **ASK 10-1**   **(07)**
    2 ...No   ⇒ **GO TO 10-2**

    1. Which of the following types of shoe advertising have you seen or heard for Kohls in the past three months **(READ LIST - CHECK ALL THAT APPLY)**.

        (08) Advertising in Sunday newspaper inserts or supplements
        (09) Advertising in the main body of the newspaper
        (10) Television advertising
        (11) Radio advertising
        (12) Billboards
        (13) Received a flier in the mail

    2. Thinking about Kohl's, what would be the <u>three</u> leading brand names of   shoes you think you would find at Kohl's?

_____   _____   _____
       (14-16)   (17-19)   (20-22)

    a. In the past year, about how many times have you been in a Kohl's shoe department? **(PROBE FOR ACTUAL NUMBER OF TIMES)**

_____TIME(S) **IF NONE -- GO TO QUESTION 11**   (23-24)

    b. On how many of those visits to Kohl's shoe department in the past year did you actually purchase shoes? **(PROBE FOR ACTUAL NUMBER OF TIMES)**

_____TIME(S) **(MUST BE LESS THAN OR EQUAL TO Q10a)**   (25-26)

11. Have you seen or heard any **shoe** advertising for Payless in the past three months, that would be since August?

    1 ...Yes ⇒ **ASK 11-1**   **(27)**
    2 ...No   ⇒ **GO TO 11-2**

    1. Which of the following types of shoe advertising have you seen or heard for Payless in the past three months **(READ LIST - CHECK ALL THAT APPLY)**.

        (28) Advertising in Sunday newspaper inserts or supplements
        (29) Advertising in the main body of the newspaper
        (30) Television advertising
        (31) Radio advertising
        (32) Billboards
        (33) Received a flier in the mail

    2. Thinking about Payless, what would be the <u>three</u> leading brand names of shoes you think you would find at Payless?

_____   _____   _____
       (34-36)   (37-39)   (40-42)

    a. In the past year, about how many times have you been in a Payless shoe store? **(PROBE FOR ACTUAL NUMBER OF TIMES)**

_____TIME(S) **IF NONE -- GO TO QUESTION 12**   (43-44)

b. On how many of those visits to Payless in the past year did you actually purchase shoes? **(PROBE FOR ACTUAL NUMBER OF TIMES)**

_____ TIME(S) **(MUST BE LESS THAN OR EQUAL TO Q11a)** (45-46)

12. Have you seen or heard any **shoe** advertising for Foot Locker in the past three months, that would be since August?

1 ...Yes ⇒ **ASK 12-1** (47)
2 ...No ⇒ **GO TO 12-2**

1. Which of the following types of shoe advertising have you seen or heard for Foot Locker in the past three months **(READ LIST - CHECK ALL THAT APPLY)**.

(48) Advertising in Sunday newspaper inserts or supplements
(49) Advertising in the main body of the newspaper
(50) Television advertising
(51) Radio advertising
(52) Billboards
(53) Received a flier in the mail

2. Thinking about Foot Locker, what would be the <u>three</u> leading brand names of shoes you think you would find at Foot Locker?

_____ _____ _____
(54-56) (57-59) (60-62)

a. In the past year, about how many times have you been in a Foot Locker shoe store? **(PROBE FOR ACTUAL NUMBER OF TIMES)**

_____ TIME(S) **IF NONE -- GO TO QUESTION 13** (63-64)

b. On how many of those visits to Foot Locker in the past year did you actually purchase shoes? **(PROBE FOR ACTUAL NUMBER OF TIMES)**

_____ TIME(S) **(MUST BE LESS THAN OR EQUAL TO Q12a)** (65-66)

13. About how many times have you been in any shoe store or shoe department since the <u>first of August</u> of this year? **(PROBE FOR ACTUAL NUMBER OF TIMES)**

_____ TIME(S) (67-68)

13a. About how many times do you think you will go to any shoe store or shoe department from now to the <u>end of next January</u>? **(PROBE FOR ACTUAL NUMBER OF TIMES)**

_____ TIME(S) (69-70)

14. Now think about visits to <u>all</u> shoe stores or shoe departments made during the <u>past 12 months</u>, on about how many of those visits did <u>you</u> actually purchase shoes for yourself or someone else? **(PROBE FOR ACTUAL NUMBER OF TIMES.)**

_____ TIME(S) **(IF NONE -- GO TO QUESTION 17)** (71-72)

a. How many <u>pairs</u> of shoes did <u>you</u> purchase in the past 12 months for yourself or someone else? **(PROBE FOR ACTUAL <u>NUMBER OF PAIRS</u>)**

_____ PAIR(S) **(MUST BE EQUAL TO OR GREATER THAN Q14)**(73-74)

5   *   *   *   *   *
(01) (02) (03) (04) (05) (06)

18

15. Of the **(ANSWER FROM Q14a)** pairs of shoes you purchased for yourself or someone else in the past 12 months, how many were dress shoes, that would be dress shoes for career and social activities; how many were comfortable casual shoes for non-athletic/leisure time activities; how many were everyday all-around leisure athletic shoes; and, how many were high-performance athletic shoes?

_____	Dress shoes	(07-08)
_____	Non-athletic casual shoes	(09-10)
_____	Athletic casual shoes	(11-12)
_____	High-performance athletic shoes	(13-14)

(TOTAL MUST EQUAL Q14a)

16. Were all these shoes for yourself or did you purchase any shoes for someone else such as a spouse, child, or someone else? **(PROBE FOR ACTUAL NUMBER OF EACH TYPE OF SHOE INDICATED IN Q15 -- TOTALS MUST EQUAL INDIVIDUAL CATEGORIES IN Q15)**

	DRESS	NON-ATHLETIC CASUAL	ATHLETIC CASUAL	HIGH-PERFORMANCE ATHLETIC
For Self	_____ (15-16)	_____ (29-30)	_____ (43-44)	_____ (57-58)
Spouse	_____ (17-18)	_____ (31-32)	_____ (45-46)	_____ (59-60)

Child (12 and Under) PROBE FOR GENDER

	DRESS	NON-ATHLETIC CASUAL	ATHLETIC CASUAL	HIGH-PERFORMANCE ATHLETIC
Boys	_____ (19-20)	_____ (33-34)	_____ (47-48)	_____ (61-62)
Girls	_____ (21-22)	_____ (35-36)	_____ (49-50)	_____ (63-64)

Child (13 and Over) PROBE FOR GENDER

	DRESS	NON-ATHLETIC CASUAL	ATHLETIC CASUAL	HIGH-PERFORMANCE ATHLETIC
Boys	_____ (23-24)	_____ (37-38)	_____ (51-52)	_____ (65-66)
Girls	_____ (25-26)	_____ (39-40)	_____ (53-54)	_____ (67-68)
Other	_____ (27-28)	_____ (41-42)	_____ (55-56)	_____ (69-70)

19. Including yourself, how many people live in your household?

WRITE IN # _____ (71)

20. How many children (under 18) do you have living at home?

WRITE IN # _____ (72)

21. And into which of the following groups do your children's ages fall? **(READ LIST -- CHECK ALL THAT APPLY.)**

❑	Less than 1 year old	(73)	❑ 13 to 15 years old	(76)
❑	1 to 5 years old	(74)	❑ 16 to 18 years old	(77)
❑	6 to 12 years old	(75)		

22. Please tell me into which of the following age group you fall? **(READ LIST)**

1...	18 to 24		5...	55 to 64	(78)
2...	25 to 34		6...	65 plus	
3...	35 to 44	**DON'T READ** 9...		REFUSED	
4...	45 to 54				

19

23.   Are you currently employed outside the home? **(PROBE FOR FULL OR PART TIME)**

              1... Employed full-time (30 + hours/week)   (07)
              2... Employed part-time (< 30 hours/week)
              3... Not employed --> **(GO TO QUESTION 25)**
DON'T READ   9... REFUSED

24.   What is your occupation?

              1 ... Professional   (08)
              2 ... White Collar
              3 ... Clerical/Office
              4 ... Sales (retail/food service)
              5 ... Blue Collar
              6 ... Teacher/counselor/clergy
              7 ... Technical
              8 ... Other/self employed

25.   What is the last level of education you completed? **(READ LIST)**

              1... High school or less   (09)
              2... Some college or vocational school
              3... College or vocational school graduate
              4... Post graduate education
DON'T READ   5... REFUSED

26.   Which of the following best describes your ethnic background? **(READ LIST)**

           1... Caucasian   4... Asian   (10)
           2... Black/Afro American   5... Native American
           3... Hispanic **DON'T READ**   9...   REFUSED

27.   Please tell me into which general category your yearly household income falls? **(READ LIST)**

           1... Under $ 20,000   6... $40,000 - $49,999   (11)
           2... $20,000 - $24,999   7... $50,000 - $74,999
           3... $25,000 - $29,999   8... $75,000 or more
           4... $30,000 - $34,999   **DON'T READ**   9... REFUSED
           5... $35,000 - $39,999

28.   What is your ZIP Code?   ___   ___   ___   ___   ___   (12-16)

RECORD SEX   1... Male   (17)
                     2... Female

THANK RESPONDENT FOR HER/HIS COOPERATION.

RECORD LENGTH OF INTERVIEW: _____ Minutes
                                   (18-19)

Consumer Product Questionnaire Example

Diaper Pail

1. Please tell me the names of all the brands of diaper pails or diaper disposal systems you can think of? **DO NOT READ LIST - MARK FIRST RESPONSE IN COLUMN Q1F, ALL OTHER RESPONSES IN COLUMN Q1M. PROBE:** Any others?

2. For which brands of diaper pails or diaper disposal systems have you seen or heard advertising? **DO NOT READ LIST - CHECK ALL THAT APPLY IN COLUMN Q2**

	Q1F First Mention	Q1M Other Mentions	Q2 Advertising
Diaper Genie 1		O	O
First Years 2		O	O
Fisher Price 3		O	O
Gerry 4		O	O
Little Tykes.................. 5		O	O
Safety First................... 6		O	O
Store Brand 7		O	O
Don't know 8		O	O
None........................... 9		O	O
Other (Specify)			
(_____)	(__)	(__)	(__)
(_____)	(__)	(__)	(__)

3. **FOR EACH BRAND MENTIONED IN Q1 (awareness) ASK**: <u>When</u> did you <u>first</u> hear about **(INSERT BRAND) - READ LIST**

   a. <u>How</u> did you <u>first</u> hear about **(INSERT BRAND) PROBE**: Any other ways?

	DIAPER GENIE	FISHER PRICE	OTHER ( )	OTHER ( )
	Q3	Q3	Q3	Q3
Within the last three months	1	1	1	1
4- 6 months ago	2	2	2	2
Over six months ago	3	3	3	3

	Q3a	Q3a	Q3a	Q3a
Magazines (PROBE)	O	O	O	O
American Baby	O	O	O	O
Baby Talk	O	O	O	O
Parenting	O	O	O	O
Parents	O	O	O	O
Child	O	O	O	O
Other Magazine (specify:_____)	O	O	O	O
Store displays	O	O	O	O
Received information in the mail	O	O	O	O
Classes/videos in class	O	O	O	O
Catalogs	O	O	O	O
Television	O	O	O	O
Relatives/Friends/neighbors/work associates	O	O	O	O
Dr./Nurse	O	O	O	O
Newspaper articles	O	O	O	O
Store advertising circulars	O	O	O	O
Childbirth instructor	O	O	O	O
Baby registries	O	O	O	O
Other (specify:_____)	O	O	O	O
Don't Know	O	O	O	O
None	O	O	O	O

4. Which method of disposing of dirty diapers do you anticipate using for your new baby? **(DO NOT READ LIST - CHECK ALL THAT APPLY)**

   1-❑ Use a diaper pail
   2-❑ Use a diaper disposal system
   3-❑ Throw them in the trash or waste can
   4-❑ Use a Diaper Genie
   5-❑ Other (please describe_____)

22

**IF RESPONDENT HAS OTHER CHILDREN "1 OR MORE IN SCREENING QUESTION B,"
ASK a, OTHERWISE GO TO Q5**

    a.   Is this different than the method used for your previous child(ren)?

        1 .. No ⇒ **GO TO Q5**

        2 .. Yes ⇒ How is it different? _____

                                     _____

                ⇒ Why are you changing? _____

                                     _____

5.   Do you currently own the diaper pail/disposal system you plan on using?

        1 ... Yes ⇒ **CONTINUE WITH a**

        2 ... No ⇒ If you were to buy one today, which brand would you buy?

                _____

                ⇒ Why would you buy this brand? _____

                        _____

                GO TO Q6

    a.   What brand is it? ❑ Diaper Genie
                                    ❑ First Years
                                    ❑ Fisher Price
                                    ❑ Gerry
                                    ❑ Little Tykes
                                    ❑ Safety First
                                    ❑ Don't know
                                    ❑ Other (specify:_____)

    b.   When did you buy or receive this diaper pail/disposal system? (**READ LIST**)

                1 .. Within the last three months
                2 .. 4- 6 months ago
                3 .. 7 months to a year ago
                3 .. 13 to 24 months ago
                5 .. Over 2 years ago
                6 .. From a previous child

c.   How did you receive your diaper pail/diaper disposal system? **(READ LIST)**

       1 ... Hand me down/bought at garage sale

       2 ... Received as a gift   ⇒ Did you request this for a gift?   1 ... Yes
                                                                    2 ... No

                                       From whom did you receive this gift?
                                       ❑ Friend/neighbor/work associate
                                       ❑ Parents (grandparents of child)
                                       ❑ Other family member

       3 ... Purchased myself or by family member not as a gift
                     ⇓

                                       Who were influential in which pail/system you purchased?
                                       ❑ Myself (mom)
                                       ❑ Spouse/husband (dad)
                                       ❑ Other family member:_____
                                       ❑ Other: _____

                                       Who was most influential?

                                       ❑ Myself (mom)
                                       ❑ Spouse (dad)
                                       ❑ Other family member:_____
                                       ❑ Other: _____

6. Thinking about the method you use to dispose of your disposable diapers, how important would you consider the following issues. **(INSERT FIRST ISSUE - START WITH CHECKED BOX)** On a 7-point scale where a 7 means the issue is extremely important and a 1 means the issue is not at all important, how important of an issue is **(REPEAT FIRST ISSUE - RECORD RATING - CONTINUE WITH REMAINING ITEMS).**

7 = Extremely Important   1 = Not at all important

- ❑ 1. _____ Safety/child proof
- ❑ 2. _____ Odor control
- ❑ 3. _____ Purchase price
- ❑ 4. _____ Manufacturer's reputation
- ❑ 5. _____ Easy to use
- ❑ 6. _____ Capacity/# of diapers it holds
- ❑ 7. _____ Durability of unit
- ❑ 8. _____ Price of bags/refills
- ❑ 9. _____ Germ control
- ❑ 10. _____ Ease of assembly

a. You mentioned that you felt **(INSERT ALL ITEMS RATED "7=EXTREMELY IMPORTANT")** were extremely important. Which <u>one</u> of these do you feel is the one most important issue? **RECORD NUMBER OF ISSUE IN SPACE BELOW.**

_____

b. Why is this the most important factor? **(PROBE FOR SPECIFICS)**

_____

_____

_____

7. Thinking about the brands of diaper pails/disposable systems you were aware of, that would be **(INSERT BRANDS MENTIONED IN Q1 - WRITE IN SPACE BELOW)**. How would you rate the performance of **(INSERT FIRST BRAND/METHOD)** on **(INSERT FIRST ITEM - START WITH CHECKED BOX)**. Would you say it was excellent, very good, good, fair, or poor. **(MARK SCALE NUMBER IN SPACE BELOW - CONTINUE WITH REMAINING ITEMS - CONTINUE WITH REMAINING METHOD/BRANDS. REPEAT SCALE AS NECESSARY).**

5 = Excellent   4 = Very Good   3 = Good   2 = Fair   1 = Poor

	(DIAPER GENIE) (_____)	(_____)
❑ Safety/child proof	_____	_____	_____
❑ Odor control	_____	_____	_____
❑ Purchase price	_____	_____	_____
❑ Manufacturer's reputation	_____	_____	_____
❑ Easy to use	_____	_____	_____
❑ Capacity/# of diapers it holds	_____	_____	_____
❑ Durability of unit	_____	_____	_____
❑ Price of bags/refills	_____	_____	_____
❑ Germ control	_____	_____	_____
❑ Ease of assembly	_____	_____	_____

a. About how much does this system cost? $____ $_____ $_____

b. Do you feel this is a good value?

1 - Excellent	1 - Excellent	1 - Excellent
2 - Good	2 - Good	2 - Good
3 - Average	3 - Average	3 - Average
4 - Poor	4 - Poor	4 - Poor

8. Which of the following best describes your current status? **(READ LIST)**

1... Married
2... Single
3... Separated/divorced/widowed
4... Not married, living with significant other

9.   Are you currently employed outside the home? **(PROBE FOR FULL OR PART TIME)**

          1...   Employed full-time (30 + hours/week)
          2...   Employed part-time (< 30 hours/week)
          3...   Not employed
DON'T READ   4...   REFUSED

10. What is the last level of education you completed? **(READ LIST)**

          1...   High school or less
          2...   Some college or vocational school
          3...   College or vocational school graduate
          4...   Post graduate education
DON'T READ   5...   REFUSED

11. Which of the following best describes your ethnic background? **(READ LIST)**

    1... White/Caucasian   4... Asian
    2... Black/African American   5... Native American
    3... Hispanic   **DON'T READ** 6... REFUSED

12. Please tell me into which general category your yearly household income falls? **(READ LIST)**

    1... Under $20,000   6... $40,000 - $49,999
    2... $20,000 - $24,999   7... $50,000 - $74,999
    3... $25,000 - $29,999   8... $75,000 or more
    4... $30,000 - $34,999   **DON'T READ** 9... REFUSED
    5... $35,000 - $39,999

13. What is your Zip Code?   ____ ____ ____ ____ ____   (12-16)

THANK RESPONDENT FOR HER PARTICIPATION

Service Questionnaire Example

Electric Utility

DATE:_____

INTERVIEWER:_____

NAME:_____

TELEPHONE:_____

Region (05)
1 ... East
2 ... Central
3 ... West

ADDRESS:_____

STATE/ZIP:_____

Customer Type (06)
    1 ... Residential
    2 ... Ag

ESTABLISH CONTACT WITH MALE/FEMALE HEAD OF HOUSEHOLD

Hello, I'm _____, calling from _____, an independent marketing research firm located in _____. We are conducting a survey on energy-related issues and would appreciate a few minutes of your time. Would this be a convenient time for you to answer a few questions? **CONTINUE WITH SURVEY OR ARRANGE CALLBACK AS APPROPRIATE.**

A.   Do you, or does anyone in your household work for a <u>power or utility company?</u>

    1 ... Yes   --> **TERMINATE AND TALLY**   (07)
    2 ... No --> **CONTINUE**

1.   Which power company supplies the electricity to your residence? **(DO NOT READ LIST)**

    1 ... Wisconsin Public Service (WPS or PSC or Pub. Service)   (08)
    2 ... Other (Please Specify)_____ **TERMINATE AND TALLY**

2.   What other power companies, or electric or gas utilities can you think of? **DO NOT READ LIST - CHECK ALL THAT APPLY.**

    (09) Wisconsin Power & Light (WP&L)
    (10) Wisconsin Electric (Wisconsin Energy)
    (11) Northern States Power (NSP)
    (12) Madison Gas & Electric (MG&E)
    (13) Con Ed
    (14) Other (Please specify)_____   _____

3.   What is the <u>primary</u> fuel source used to heat your home? **READ LIST - ALLOW ONLY ONE RESPONSE.**
    (15)   (16)
    1 ... Natural gas --> **ASK:** what company supplies your natural gas? 1 ...WPSC
    2 ... Oil   2 ...Other
    3 ... Electric
    4 ... Wood
    5 ... LP gas
    6 ... Other

4a. I am going to read you a list of items. For each item, please tell me if you feel you are getting your money's worth for the cost of that item? We will use a 7-point scale where a 7 means you are definitely getting your money's worth and a 1 means you are definitely not getting your money's worth. The first item is (**READ FIRST ITEM - ROTATE LIST STARTING WITH CHECKED BOX - REPEAT SCALE AS NECESSARY - CONTINUE WITH REMAINING ITEMS. MARK RESPONSE IN SPACE UNDER COLUMN A**)

SCALE   7 = *Definitely getting money's worth*   1 = *Definitely <u>not</u> getting money's worth*

A		B			
Current Value Rating		Improve	Stay The Same	Get Worse	Don't Know
(17)❑ ___Groceries		1	2	3	0	(24)
(18)❑ ___Electricity		1	2	3	0	(25)
(19)❑ ___Clothing		1	2	3	0	(26)
(20)❑ ___Telephone Service		1	2	3	0	(27)
(21)❑ ___Home Heating		1	2	3	0	(28)
(22)❑ ___Cable TV		1	2	3	0	(29)
(23)❑ ___Gasoline		1	2	3	0	(30)

4b. Considering these same items, do you think the value for your money you will be getting for these items will improve, stay the same, or get worse in the next few years? **READ ITEMS AND MARK RESPONSE IN COLUMN B ABOVE - REPEAT SCALE AS NECESSARY.**

5. I am going to read you some statements about the utility that provides you with electricity. For each statement, please tell me if you strongly agree, agree, neither agree nor disagree, disagree, or strongly disagree. The first item is (**READ ITEM - ROTATE LIST STARTING WITH CHECKED BOX - REPEAT SCALE AS NECESSARY - CONTINUE WITH REMAINING ITEMS.**

SCALE   5 = *Strongly agree*   3 = *Neither agree nor disagree*   1 = *Strongly disagree*
             4 = *Agree*   2 = *Disagree*   0 = *Don't know*

(31)❑ ___ Your electric utility is an efficient producer of energy?

(32)❑ ___ Your electric utility encourages you to conserve energy?

(33)❑ ___ Your electric utility is a leader in economic development?

(34)❑ ___ Your electric utility is a leader in the state in terms of providing information on energy-related issues?

(35)❑ ___ Your electric utility is an innovator of energy products and services?

(36)❑ ___ Your electric utility is a socially responsible company concerned about the environment?

(37)❑ ___ If I could choose any electric utility to provide my electricity, I would choose my current electric utility company?

(38)❑ ___ My electric utility provides education to Wisconsin residents on energy conservation and related issues.

(39)❑ ___ My electric utility is invloved and supports the local community.

(40)❑ ___ My electric utility is a leader in high-technology energy products and services.

6. Are you familiar with any rebate or other energy efficiency programs offered by your <u>electric</u> utility company?

   1 ... No --> **GO TO Q7**   (41)
   2 ... Yes   --> **CONTINUE WITH Q 6a**

   a. Could you briefly describe these programs **(PROBE FOR DETAILS - CLARIFY VAGUE RESPONSES)**

      _____ (42-43)

      _____ (44-45)

      _____ (46-47)

   b. Would you say these programs have exceeded your expectations, met your expectations, or have not met your expectations in terms of your ability to conserve energy?

      1 ... Exceeded my expectations   (48)
      2 ... Met my expectations
      3 ... Have not met my expectations

   c. Would you say these programs have exceeded your expectations, met your expectations, or have not met your expectations in terms of reducing your cost for energy?

      1 ... Exceeded my expectations   (49)
      2 ... Met my expectations
      3 ... Have not met my expectations

7. What, if any, advantages do you feel energy efficiency programs offered by utilities provide <u>you</u>?**(PROBE FOR DETAILS - CLARIFY VAGUE RESPONSES)**

      _____ (50-51)

      _____ (52-53)

      _____ (54-55)

8. Do you remeber seeing, hearing or receiving any advertising from your electric utility company in the past six (6) months?

   1 ... Yes -->   **ASK a**   (56)
   2 ... No -->   **GO TO Q9**

a. Where did you see or hear this advertising **(READ LIST - CHECK ALL THAT APPLY)**

  (57) Television
  (58) Radio
  (59) Newspapers
  (60) Received in the mail
    (61) In your bill
    (62) In separate mailing
  (63) Billboards
  (64) Other (Please Specify)_____

b. Can you briefly tell me what you remember about this advertising?

  _____
                                                          (65-66)(67-68)
  _____
                                                          (69-70)

9. There is some talk that in the near future, you may be able to choose your power company just like you can choose your long distance telephone company. Would you like to be able to have the choice of which company supplies your power?

  1 ... Yes   (71)
  2 ... No
  3 ... Don't know

  a. Do you feel having such a choice will have the effect of lowering your utility bills, raising your utility bills, or have no effect on your utility bills?

    1 ... Raise utility bill   (72)
    2 ... Lower utility bill
    3 ... No effect on utility bill
    4 ... Don't know

  b. Do you feel having such a choice will have a positive, negative or no effect on the service provided to you by the power company?

    1 ... Positive effect   (73)
    2 ... Negative effect
    3 ... No effect on service
    4 ... Don't know

31

10. Which of the following statements would best agree with your feelings?

A   1 ... Bigger utilities are able to provide power at a lower cost   (74)
    2 ... Smaller utilities are able to provide power at a lower cost

B. 1 ... Bigger utilities are better able to minimize the effect of power outages.   (75)
    2 ... Smaller utilities are better able to minimize the effect of power outages.

C. 1 ... Bigger utilities are able to provide better local service to customers.   (76)
    2 ... Smaller utilities are able to provide better local service to customers.

D. 1 ... Bigger utilities are better able to provide you with more products and services which allow
          you to use energy wisely and effeciently in building a new home(farm) or remodeling and
          updating an existing home(farm).   (77)

    2 ... Smaller utilities are better able to provide you with more products and services which allow
          you to use energy wisely and effeciently in building a new home(farm) or remodeling and
          updating an existing home(farm).

                                                                        2   *   *   *.
                                                                      (01)(02)(03)(04)

11. In newspapers across the state, Wisconsin Public Service publishes a weekly column called the
    Energy Exchange. This column features questions and answers on energy efficiency and
    conservation matters. It features a picture of a Wisconsin Public Service consumer consultant. Do
    you recall seeing such a column in a newspaper in the past year?

    1 ... Yes   --> **CONTINUE WITH a**   (05)
    2 ... No --> **GO TO Q12**

    a. Which of the following statements best describes your readership of this weekly column?

        1 ...   I've seen the column, but have not read it   (06)
        2 ...   I've seen the column and occasionally skim it
        3 ...   I've seen the column and occasionally read it
        4 ...   I've seen the column and read it often

    b. What specific topics or hints can you recall seeing in the column?

        _____
                                                                        (07-08)(09-10)

        _____
                                                                        (11-12)(13-14)
    c. On a scale from 1 to 7, with 1 being poor and 7 being excellent, how would you rate the
        usefulness of the Energy Exchange Column?

        Poor   1   2   3   4   5   6   7   Excellent   (15)

12. Do you own or rent your current residence?   1 ... Own   (16)
                                                   2 ... Rent

13. How long have you lived in the State of Wisconsin? _____ yrs.   (17-18)

14 Including yourself, how many people live in your household?

         WRITE IN # ____   (19)

15. Please tell me into which of the following age group you fall? **(READ LIST)**

    1... 18 to 24   5... 55 to 64   (20)
    2... 25 to 34   6... 65 plus
    3... 35 to 44   **DON'T READ   9...REFUSED**
    4... 45 to 54

16. What is the last level of education you completed? **(READ LIST)**

         1... High school or less   (21)
         2... Some college or vocational school
         3... College or vocational school graduate
         4... Post graduate education
    DON'T READ 9... REFUSED

17. Are you currently employed outside the home? **(PROBE FOR FULL OR PART TIME)**

         1... Employed full-time (30 + hours/week)   (22)
         2... Employed part-time (< 30 hours/week)
         3... Not employed --> **(GO TO QUESTION 16)**
    DON'T READ 9... REFUSED

18. What is your occupation? _____   (23)

19. Please tell me into which general category your yearly household income falls? **(READ LIST)**

          1...   Under $ 20,000   (24)
          2... $20,000 - $29,999
          3... $30,000 - $39,999
          4... $40,000 - $49,999
          5... $50,000 - $74,999
          6... $75,000 or more

DON'T READ   9...   REFUSED

20. What is your ZIP Code?   ___   ___   ___   ___   ___   (25-29)

RECORD GENDER OF RESPONDENT   1... Male   (30)
                                         2... Female

THANK RESPONDENT FOR HER/HIS COOPERATION.

RECORD LENGTH OF INTERVIEW: _____   Minutes
                                  (31-32)

CHAPTER 2

HOW TO PREPARE A BUSINESS REVIEW

Chapter Objectives

1. Define the following:

   — Business Scope

   — Core Competency

   — Marketing Capability

   — Penetration

   — All Commodity Volume (ACV)

   — Price Elasticity

   — Brand Development Index (BDI)

   — Category Development Index (CDI)

2. Review the three business review steps and their component tasks, as outlined in the text:

   Step 1: Scope

   — Strengths and weaknesses

   — Core competencies

   — Marketing Capabilities

   — Develop Options

   — Analysis of Options

   Step 2: Product and Market Review

   — Corporate Philosophy/Description of the Company

   — Product Analysis

— Category and Company Sales Trends

— Behavior Trends

— Distribution

— Pricing

— Competitive Review

Step 3: Target Market Effectors

— Target Market Segments

— Product Awareness and Attributes

— Trial and Retrial Behavior

3. Discuss the key marketing issues and questions that need to be answered in each of the business review steps.

4. Provide students insight as to the data requirements and material that needs to be analyzed in order to answer the above questions.

5. Provide students a format with which they can write succinct summary statements describing the findings.

Teaching Suggestions

At a minimum, review the questions to be addressed and charts for each of the business review steps. In addition, review each step with students, using the following suggestions for discussion.

Step 1: Scope

Determining the scope of the business up front provides the boundaries and direction for the plan, and helps provide structure to the information needed in the business review. Review the scope case study with students. Discuss the potential scopes of the students' businesses, if this is an applications course. Provide examples, including consumer products firms, service firms, and business-to-business or industrial firms, and discuss the scopes of these businesses. Alternatively, discuss the scope of the students' career aspirations.

Task 1: Provide an overview of company strengths and weaknesses (pp. 30–31)

Review with the students the definitions of strengths and weaknesses on p. 30. Use the case example provided in the text or come up with another example to identify strengths and weaknesses.

Task 2: Identify Core Competencies (pp. 31–32)

The concept of a core competency can be a difficult one to grasp. Provide examples for students to discuss, applying the "litmus test" provided on p. 32. A core competency must:

— Make a significant contribution to the perceived customer benefit of the end product.

— Be difficult for competitors to imitate.

Task 3: Identify marketing capabilities (pp. 32–33)

What are the advantages a company has within the marketing mix? Again, discuss with students the marketing capabilities of their businesses.

Task 4: Develop potential business scope options (pp. 33–36)

Using your same example, develop and discuss alternative scope options. Review the implications of each approach.

Task 5: Analysis of your options (pp. 36–38)

Use the format of the chart provided in Appendix B of the text to analyze each scope option.

Class Discussion/Questions

1. What determines a company's business scope? What are the components?

2. What is a core competency? Discuss examples of companies and their core competencies.

3. What are the Marketing Capabilities of the students' firms?

Step 2: Product and Market Review

Task 1: Corporate Philosophy/Description of the Company (pp. 39–41)

Different companies are unique in the ways they do business, their historical backgrounds and their organizational structure—all of which have some level of impact on the development of a marketing plan. It is important for marketers to briefly describe, up front, predetermined corporate objectives, pertinent company and product history, along with product information. This information can be obtained through reviewing company business plans, training manuals, trade journal articles, 10-k financial reports, and interviewing corporate officers and managers. It is often a good idea for marketers to use a combination of written sources and verbal interviewing to determine if there is a discrepancy between what is written and what the employees are actually saying about the company.

The first task is divided into three main sections: corporate goals and objectives; general company history; and organizational structure. Use the questions at the end of each section in the book to provide an overview as to the type of information that is expected from this section.

This section is a good place to provide the students with an overview of the differences between the four basic types of businesses discussed in this book—package goods, retail, service, and business to business. Following is an example of a retail organizational chart and a consumer package goods organizational chart. Note the major differences:

— The brand manager marketing orientation of the consumer package goods company.

— The heavy influence of the merchandise department in the retail organization.

At this point you might want to discuss the similarities and difference of consumer consumer package goods companies with consumer retail companies and the differences between consumer marketing companies and business-to-business firms. The following list will help structure this discussion.

Retail Organizational Chart

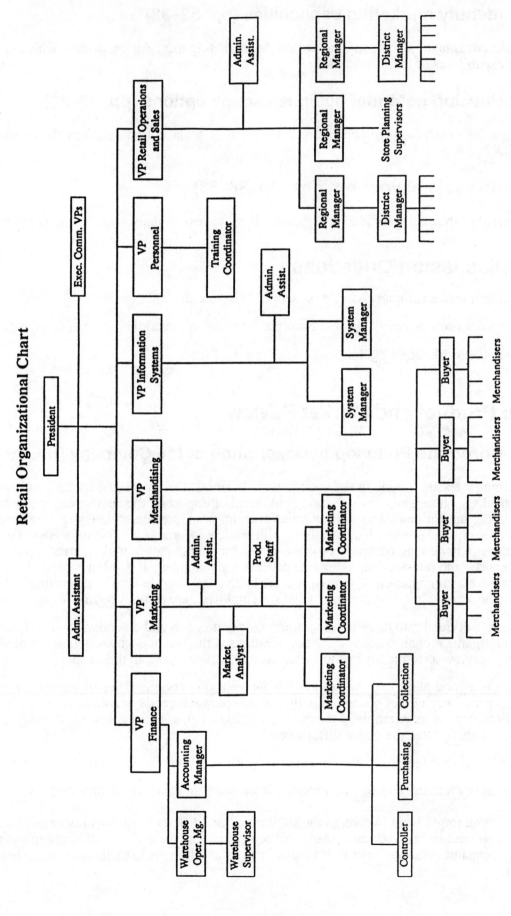

Package Goods Organizational Chart

Board of Directors

Chief Executive Officer

Research & Development
- VP R & D
  - Labs

Operations

Executive VP

VP Product Group Manager
- Product Manager
- Product Manager
- Product Manager

Executive VP

VP Product Group Manager
- Product Manager
- Product Manager
- Product Manager

VP Administration

Corporate Staff VP

Engineering
Corporate Services
Finance
Government Relations
Legal
Personnel
Public Relations
International
VP Marketing

Sales
- Divisions
- Divisions
- Divisions

Similarities Between Retail and Package Goods Companies

Both sell a product to consumers and thus:

— have to develop a consumer franchise of loyal customers who do repeat business.

— have to market products to consumers or purchasers of their products.

— utilize mass media to market to consumers.

— have a need to understand the consumers' awareness, attitudes and behavior patterns toward the product.

— have to do a good job of in-store or point-of-purchase merchandising.

— use promotions (package goods to force distribution to the trade and directly to consumers and retail to generate customer traffic).

— require feedback as to how the business is doing. Thus the MIS (management information systems) department is critical to the business.

— have to manage personnel.

— both have a strong need for a strong financial department.

Differences Between Retail and Package Goods Companies

— In package goods marketing the primary focus is on the product. However, for the retailer, equal importance is paid to the product, the location, and the people (from the store manager to the sales staff).

— Package goods marketers have to be concerned with gaining and maintaining distribution. Retailers own their own distribution outlets. Thus while the initial location strategy is important, distribution does not require the daily attention for the retailer as it does for the package good marketer.

— Retailers in general have more products to sell and a much broader mix of products to market than package goods companies.

— Package goods marketers have a more standardized national or regional environment. In retail, it is difficult to standardize the product and location from store to store and market to market.

— Retailers typically have unique trading areas with target market preferences changing from one trading area to another. Each store therefore has to address a localized target market and meet the local target's needs.

— Retail focuses more on the short term. A promotion that ran over the weekend can be analyzed for results by Monday.

— In general package goods companies focus on long-term brand building while retailers focus on short-term promotion.

— Because of the short-term focus, retailers must act upon and sometimes overreact to short-term retail sales environment. Retailers are more apt to adjust strategy after a week of down sales than are package goods marketers.

— There is a better quantifiable database for package goods marketers than for retail marketers. Firms like Nielsen (information about sales and product movement at the grocery shelf level) and SAMI (information about product movement from the warehouse) or Behavior Scan (information about customers' demographics, viewing habits and sales) are readily available to package goods marketers. Information for retailers must be developed by the retailer through primary research and sale tracking at cash registers.

— Local trends affect retailers more than package goods companies. The retailer has to be able to tailor its product mix, location strategy, media strategy, merchandising, pay scales, point-of-purchase displays, sales strategy, and pricing to the local market.

— Package goods companies, in most cases, market a product they manufactured or had exclusively manufactured for them. Retail companies, in most cases, market a product some other company manufactured. Thus the merchandising and buying function is critical for retailers and the manufacturing process is critical for manufacturers. In addition, manufacturers have complete control over the product they ultimately sell. Retailers often do not have control because they most often purchase product from manufacturers.

— Retailers have direct control over the in-store signage. Package goods companies can sell in-store via messages on product packaging but have no direct control over point-of-purchase displays and signage. However, because of the large number of in-store purchase decisions, package goods companies spend a great deal of time trying to convince the grocer, for example, to utilize their point-of-purchase materials.

— There is more of a price orientation with retailers. In most cases the manufacturer creates the image and the retailer sells the product. Stated another way, manufacturers create demand and retailers sell product mix and price offering to consumers.

— Retailers have to advertise what is for sale and <u>where</u> the consumer can buy the product. Package goods firms focus primarily on selling their product.

— Retailers usually sell only to the consumer. However, package goods firms usually have two target markets, trade and consumer.

Differences Between Business-to-Business and Consumer Companies

— The target market for business-to-business companies are other businesses or commercial enterprises and not individual consumers. <u>OEMs</u>, original equipment manufacturers, purchase equipment to use in the manufacturing of their product; <u>industrial distributors</u> sell products to other middlemen, OEMs, government or institutional organizations, or the ultimate individual consumer.

— There are often fewer customers in business-to-business marketing than in consumer marketing. However, business-to-business customers tend to be larger in size (dollar volume or purchase quantity).

— The business-to-business distribution system is typically more direct than the consumer marketing organization. It often includes either a wholly-owned manufacturer's field sales division or independent manufacturer's reps who are responsible for selling the product to the target market. In either case, there is usually a more direct channel of distribution to the buyer than in consumer marketing, with fewer independent middlemen such as wholesalers.

— The business-to-business customer tends to be more motivated by cost considerations such as profit, bottom line, and meeting expense objectives. The purchase is usually more objective than subjective. The customer must often justify the purchase in terms of measurable results to management, something completely foreign to a consumer purchase process.

— There is often a competitive bidding process that business-to-business firms must undertake in order to receive an order. In addition, there is widespread use of trade discounts off list price. Negotiated pricing is also common with sophisticated agents wielding powerful influence.

— The demand for business-to-business products is often derived from consumer demand. Thus the business-to-business marketer must monitor both his direct customers (businesses making purchases) and the individual consumers who are creating the demand for the product.

— Business-to-business products are usually more technical and require greater servicing and technical selling. There needs to be a long-term commitment to the purchaser.

— For business-to-business firms, products are sometimes purchased for inventories rather than for immediate use. While the average household has a pantry and occasionally stocks up on common household products, this does not compare to businesses that hold large inventories in warehouses.

— Business-to-business firms use utilitarian packaging, focusing on protecting the product rather than promoting the product.

— Personnel selling is more important in business-to-business marketing and there is less emphasis on mass media and marketing techniques. Advertising that does exist is more technical and informational on its orientation.

— Price promotion is not used as often in business-to-business as in consumer marketing.

One final note. Remember that this is an overview chapter. In application or case courses, don't let students spend too much time on this step. It's important but not at the exclusion of the other chapters. It's easy to overlook that there are many other steps. Don't spend too much time on this softer "corporate culture" material at the expense of the other steps.

Class Discussion/Questions

1. Discuss how one company's goals and objectives might differ from those of another company selling the same product. (The age of the company makes a difference. A young company might be growth oriented and focused on increasing sales while an established company might be interested in competing against another company for increased market share or in maintaining market share in an increasingly competitive marketplace.)

2. Why is it important to understand a company's product history? How can this help the marketer in the marketing of the company and the product?

3. In the discussion above, service firms were not compared. Where would they fit? How are they similar and different to the other types of companies discussed?

4. Is marketing the same whether it be for a retail, package goods, service, or business-to-business firm? What are the major similarities and differences?

Task 2: Product Analysis (pp. 41–44)

While Task 1 looks into the company history and structure, the second task looks at the history and structure of the product category. This task is divided into four sections. First, you must identify the products within the determined business scope. Second, review the product offering of the company. Third, review the product offerings of the competition. Finally, review trends within the product category. Each of these steps is outlined on pp. 42 and 43. Use examples to discuss each with students.

Class Discussion/Questions

Using the student's firms or products as examples, discuss the scope of their business. What are their product offerings within that scope? What are the competitors? Discuss the strengths and weaknesses of the students' firms' product offerings versus those of their competition.

Task 3: Category and Company Sales Trends (pp. 44–48)

Sales data can be analyzed in many ways. The purpose of this section is to teach students how to look at sales numbers from a relationship standpoint (comparing one set of numbers with another). It also provides students a framework with which to analyze the sales of any given business by starting broad with total sales of the industry, company, and competition; and then getting narrower by looking at sales by department or brand. Finally, the step provides a methodology for determining market share and demonstrates how to plot seasonality of sales and sales by geographic territory or target market segment. A note for retail-oriented classes: page 45 discusses store-for-store sales.

Here is a suggested method for reviewing this section.

Discuss the importance of using reference points when reviewing sales. Typical examples follow.

The fact that the Mead Company has sales of $170MM means very little. What is meaningful is the following:

— The Mead Company has sales of $170MM. It ranks third in the category with the top two companies generating sales of between $230MM and $250MM. Three other companies have sales between $125MM and $150MM. These six companies account for approximately 85% of the cottage sales.

— The Mead Company has experienced average sales increases of 3% annually over the last five years. The market has experienced an average of 8% sales increase over the past five years. In addition, The Mead Company has experienced a decrease in market share while the top two companies in the category have been gaining market share.

— The Mead Company has two brands. Widgets, which account for 70% of the sales volume, have been flat over the past five years. Gidgets, which account for 30% of the volume, have increased 10%. However, nationally, Gidgets (which account for 20% of the sales) have been flat and Widgets (which account for 80% of the sales) have increased around 8% per year.

— The Mead Company has flat seasonality, no one month stands out from another. However, the category experiences strong sales throughout the year with peaks during the June to July and winter holiday seasons.

— Sales skew heavily toward the North Central part of the United States. There is very little sales volume in the South.

With this information the marketer can start making judgments that will later affect the marketing plan:

— The category is dominated by two leaders. This means that these two companies have marketing resources for product development, advertising, media, and promotions beyond the other companies in the field. One way to view this data and later approach this situation in the marketing plan is to develop niches. The Mead Company most likely will not be able to go head to head with the leaders but must look for innovative ways to beat the leaders in particular segments. The Mead Company could, for example, specialize in a particular customer segment, specialize with a specific brand, or dominate one advertising medium that the competition does not.

— The Mead Company is performing below that of the market. One reason might be that the Mead Company has performed below that of the category with Widgets, the brand that accounts for the majority of the sales nationally and which has had the strongest growth rate nationally. The company must make a decision to determine why sales are lagging for the Widgets or determine if there is a large enough market in Gidgets and if Mead can further capitalize in its strength in this area, thus capturing the majority market share for this brand.

— The Mead Company must determine why the category experiences strong seasonal sales increases at specific times of the year while it doesn't. Then plans need to be developed to take advantage of this occurrence.

— The Mead Company must determine why sales skew to the North Central part of the country. Then a strategic decision must be made whether to continue to emphasize and take further advantage of the strategic strength of their geographical segment or to target another potential area for growth.

Next, discuss each of the five sales data categories (pages 44-47). Start with the questions that should be addressed on pages 47-48. Then discuss Exhibits 2-2 through 2-5 as methodologies for answering the questions.

Class Discussion/Questions

1. Why is it important to compare the company's sales data with the category's sales data? What type of information does this provide the marketer?

2. A marketing manager should break out total company and category sales into sales by department or brand. Discuss the types of information this procedure can provide the marketer and the type of action plan that could result from these findings.

3. Assume that you discover that your company' sales have a strong seasonality skew to the months of September to October and March to April. You also discover that your company is relatively weak during the rest of the year. How could you use this information? (Additional information on the category's seasonality would be needed for a comparison against the company's monthly sales. If there was a month that the category did well and your company didn't, find out why and then target that month for growth. Don't try to increase periods when consumers don't naturally buy. First make sure the company dominates periods of time when consumers are buying in the category. Consider diversifying into other product areas to increase down months.)

4. Why is it important to determine sales trends by geographic territory or by customer segments? What decisions can a marketer make based upon this information?

Task 4: Behavior Trends (pp. 48–55)

As much as the disciplined marketing planning process attempts to provide a highly-structured and quantifiable format for determining and planning an organization's marketing activities, it is ultimately consumer behavior that determines its success or failure -- whether people visit a retailer, purchase a product, repurchase, purchase a certain volume, etc. Even behavior not directly related to purchase can have an impact on an organization's ability to effectively market its product or service. Related to consumer behavior is "business behavior" trends, such as downsizing, outsourcing, etc. Such behavior can be difficult to predict -- we are talking about people after all. Therefore, a thorough understanding of consumer and business behavior, and analysis of consumer trends, is an extremely important component of the marketing planning process.

Use the examples provided in the text and the students' businesses to discuss implications of the various types of trends on specific categories and potential decisions. Review the Questions to be Addressed under each section, and apply to the students' businesses or other examples. Use some of the other books mentioned in the text to stimulate discussion, including Naisbitt's *Megatrends 2000,* or Popcorn's *The Popcorn Report.*

The major objective of this section is to have students understand the importance of trends in daily life and the world in which they live, and the implications they have on marketing decision-making and planning. In addition, they should begin to form conclusions regarding the various types of trends and how they might affect their assigned product or service in any element of the marketing mix. This can be a fun discussion.

Class Discussion/Questions

1. A major demographic trend is the growing number of elderly. What are some potential implications of this trend for a marketer? Discuss based on the students' product or service.

2. What is a growing trend among Fortune 500 companies? As above, what are some potential marketing implications of this trend?

3. What are some significant social or consumer trends? What are the implications for your firm or for an example business?

4. The rapid increase in the use of home computers and the worldwide web is a technological , consumer and media trend. What are the implications for retailers?

Task 5: Distribution (pp. 55–65)

Distribution is the method of delivering the product to the consumer. In a business review, students aim to determine which method of distribution is used most successfully by the industry, the company, and the competitors. However, the concept of distribution varies depending upon the type of business category. That is why this task is divided into four sections: retail; package goods; business-to-business; and service.

The penetration portion of the retail section should be discussed in class. Reproduce an overhead transparencies the charts on pages 57 and 58. Work through the numbers using the examples on page 58. Keep the following in mind when explaining these charts.

— The estimated number of households can be found in a SRDS or Nielsen DMA Test Market Profile Book.

— The advertising plans portion of the chart was put in to help the marketer determine how the optimum number of stores would affect the company's ability to leverage media dollars. In most cases the optimal number of stores provides a large enough sales base to allow for efficient levels of advertising.

— The 5% of sales number is an average used for demonstration purposes. Actual company advertising to sales ratios may vary substantially.

The Market Coverage section of the Package Goods section should also be discussed in class. The concept of ACV (all commodity volume) is important and we suggest going over Exhibit 2.9 in class on the board or on overhead.

Class Discussion/Questions

1. Why are media costs included in the store penetration analysis for retail stores? (One of the main reasons a retailer wants to penetrate a market is to leverage media and advertising costs across more stores. That's also why markets are defined by DMAs or television viewing areas.)

2. Is ACV defined in terms of just your product category or all grocery store volume? (All grocery store volume is defined by a grouping of common products.)

3. When should a business-to-business firm go direct? When should it use independent reps or wholesalers and distributors? (See Chapter 12.)

Task 6: Pricing (pp. 65-68)

Price is a prominent part of the marketing decision-making process and an area that the students will most likely have little background. The problem with pricing decisions is that there are no real answers that are right or wrong. A price that is too high may discourage purchase of the product and encourage competition in the form of lower price and more entries into the product category. Alternatively, a price that is too low may be a deterrent to reaching profit and sales goals.

The business review section on pricing is designed to provide the students with pricing data relative to competition, changes in the marketplace price structure, and strengths of consumer demand. This information will provide a reference and help guide your pricing objectives and strategies in the subsequent marketing plan.

This section focuses on four main topics: the price of the students' company or brand relative to the competition; the distribution of sales by price point relative to the competition; the price elasticity of the students' product or brand; and the cost structure of the product.

If the class has an application or case orientation, encourage students to actually go out and "shop' their own product and those of the competition, recording information similar to that recorded in Exhibit 2.10 on page 66. (Even if yours is the more traditional marketing management course, assignment of a product and product category can be the basis for an out-of-class exercise.) Make sure students visit as many stores or outlets and as many different categories of stores as possible. For example, if student groups are preparing a business review for facial tissues, have them gather pricing and competitive pricing information from local grocery stores, chain grocery stores, convenience stores and mass merchandisers. Often pricing trends can be segmented by the type of outlet category.

Next have students break out the distribution of sales by price point as is demonstrated in Exhibit 2.11 on page 67. This is known as determining price lines. There is often a positive correlation between certain price points and consumers'; perception of quality and value. Therefore, many product categories have established natural price segments. In the consumers' mind, each price line is related to the price line preceding it and following it. Price lines tend to provide consumers information about product quality, thus reducing confusion and helping to facilitate the purchase decision process.

If the percent of sales for any particular price line is not available, have students "project" the figure by using information gathered in the shopping trips. Staying with the facial tissue example, students could estimate and record the amount of shelf space each major price point of facial tissue accounts for in the stores. In this example, students could assume that shelf space equates to sales.

Elasticity will be hard to determine without going into complicated economic models, testing programs, or being able to change the product price over a period of time and tracing the effect on demand. Students don't usually have an opportunity to do this. The best way for the students to get a feel for the price elasticity of their products is to interview store managers to get their reaction. Additionally, have them discuss the issue with marketing personnel connected with the marketing of the company's product. In this manner, two separate sources can serve as input, the company and the distribution point. The answers should be similar but a reconciliation between discrepancies will have to be made if they are not.

Finally, have students determine the cost structure for their product. Theoretically, price is determined by the sales dollars needed to cover the cost of goods sold, operating expenses, and profit after taxes. Of course one other element is needed, projected volume or units sold. (The greater the volume, the greater the amount of dollars to cover fixed costs. Smaller volume companies usually require greater margins.) If the cost structure is not available to the students and they cannot project one based upon industry averages, provide them with the following or something relative to their product category:

— Cost of goods sold: 55% of the sales price

— Selling expense: 20% of the sales price

— General administrative expense: 10% of the sales price

— 15% net income (before tax and retained earnings distribution)

The major focus of this section is to have students gather price information for their assigned case or out-of-class assignment so that they are aware of the pricing structure of a product relative to the competition. In addition, they should form conclusions as to:

— The price sensitivity.

— Whether natural pricing segments exist.

— Which segments account for the most demand.

— The consumer within the target markets who shop the different price segments.

— Whether there are different target market segments shopping different price ranges.

Make sure students understand why they are gathering this information. The price of a product is meaningless to consumers unless they compare it to another price for a similar product or some other purchase choice. The business review's purpose is to force the students to gather pricing information that allows them to understand their product's price structure relative to the competition's, how consumers purchase the product category in terms of price categories, the impact of price changes on the purchase of the product category, and the final cost structure of the product.

Make sure students understand why they are gathering this information. The price of a product is meaningless to consumers unless they compare it to another price for a similar product or some other purchase choice. The business review's purpose is to force the students to gather pricing information that allows them to understand their product's price structure relative to the competition's, how consumers purchase the product category in terms of price categories, the impact of price changes on the purchase of the product category, and the final cost structure of the product.

Class Discussion/Questions

1. Give advantages/disadvantages of a high, or premium, price policy.

2. What are the drawbacks of constantly changing price to match the competition and/or changes in season demand?

3. List some products that have price inelastic demand. How does a marketer market differently for these products versus those that have elastic demand?

4. How do you determine breakeven?

Task 7: Competitive Review (pp. 69–73)

The competitive analysis section is designed to provide students with a summary of how the company they are studying is performing relative to the competition across key marketing variables. This step forces students to consider strategic and tactical differences and similarities between how the company markets its products versus how the competition markets their products.

The major force of the chapter is the questions section on pages 70 and 73 and Exhibit 2.13 on page 72. Have the students complete the exhibit as completely as possible for their company or product.

Two media spending analysis examples follow. The first one could apply to a retail or package goods company. The second example looks at a bank and its competitors. While this is only one part of the competitive spending section, it can serve as a discussion starter to the media ramifications from analyzing competitive spending.

Competitive Spending Example 1

Retail or Package Goods

Company	TV $(000)	Radio $(000)	Outdoor $(000)	Newspaper $(000)	Total $(000)
1st Quarter					
X	14.6	0.0	0.0	38.0	52.6
Y	22.7	2.0	0.0	15.0	39.7
Z	12.1	12.0	50.0	75.0	149.1
Total	49.4	14.0	50.0	128.0	241.4
2nd Quarter					
X	15.6	0.0	0.0	50.0	65.6
Y	15.0	0.0	0.0	20.0	35.0
Z	10.0	15.0	60.0	50.0	175.0
Total	40.6	15.0	60.0	120.0	235.6
3rd Quarter					
X	20.0	10.0	20.0	60.0	110.0
Y	15.0	2.0	0.0	20.0	37.0
Z	8.0	10.0	50.0	40.0	10.0
Total	43.0	22.0	70.0	120.0	255.0
4th Quarter					
X	30.6	0.0	0.0	40.0	70.6
Y	20.0	10.0	5.0	30.0	52.0
Z	10.0	15.0	50.0	800.0	155.0
Total	60.6	25.0	55.0	150.0	277.6

— Company Z dominates spending.

— While not dominating total spending, Company X has strategically decided to dominate television spending. If you can't be the spending leader, it is smart to dominate a medium so that your company dominates share of voice in one important medium.

— From these data, seasonality of spending could be determined.

— Company X increases spending dramatically during the 3rd quarter. What would be the potential reasons for this? (Possible reasons include leading into the important 4th quarter, and a product line that has a strong back-to-school correlation.)

Competitive Spending Example 2

Bank

Total Market Expenditures

by Quarter 1995 and 1996

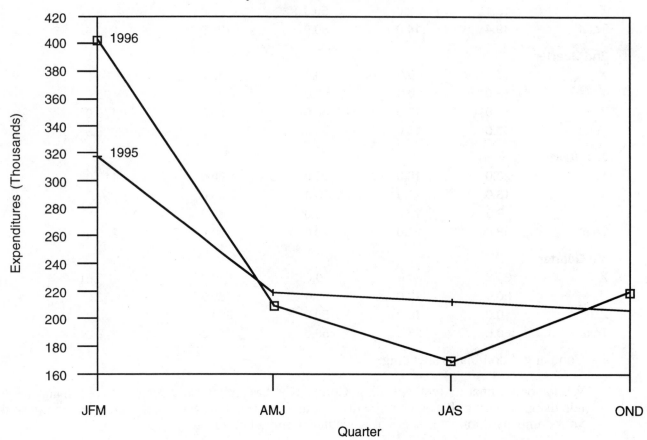

Total Market

1996 Expenditures by Medium

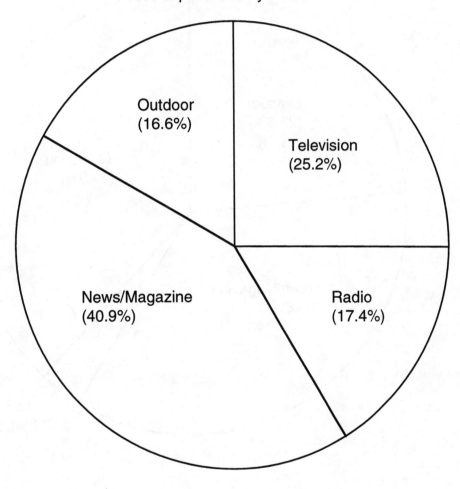

Bank A

1996 Expenditures by Medium

Outdoor
(23.8%)

Television
(39.0%)

News/Magazine
(33.6%)

Radio
(3.6%)

Bank A

1995 Expenditures by Medium

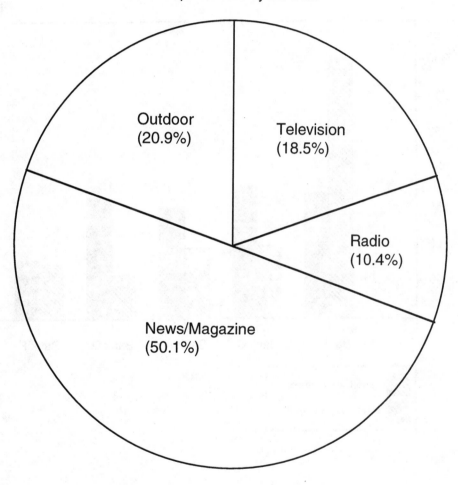

Outdoor
(20.9%)

Television
(18.5%)

Radio
(10.4%)

News/Magazine
(50.1%)

Top Six Advertisers

Expenditures 1995 and 1996

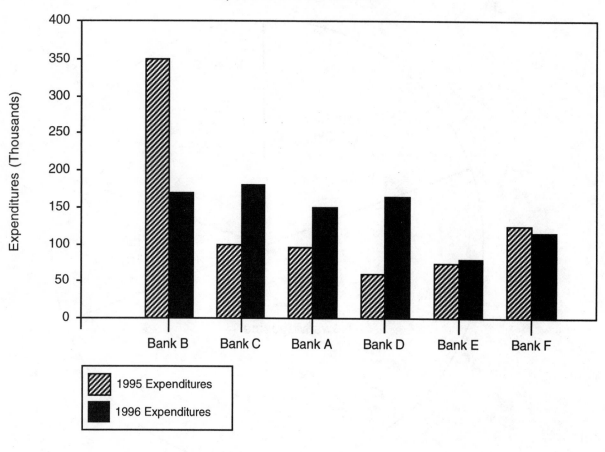

Expenditures by Medium

The 1996 expenditures by medium are divided as follows:

Television   Bank A had the greatest share of the market's television spending, accounting for 25% with 59.4M. The next closest competitors were Bank D and Bank F, with 16% of the television spending.

Bank A	24%
Bank D	16
Bank F	16
Bank B	15
Bank C	11
Bank G	11

Radio   Bank D had the greatest share of spending in radio, accounting for 28% with $48.7M. Bank B followed closely behind with 22% of the spending. Each remaining competitor accounted for less than 10% of the total radio dollars, with Bank A accounting for 3%.

Bank D	28%
Bank B	22
Bank E	9
Bank H	8
Bank C	8
Bank I	8

Newspaper/Magazine   The leading spender in newspapers/magazines was Bank C with $91.8M, or 23% share of spending. The next closest spending competitors were Bank D and Bank E, with 16% and 15% share of spending, respectively. Bank A accounted for 13% of the spending.

Bank C	23%
Bank D	16
Bank E	15
Bank A	13
Bank B	12

Outdoor   The outdoor category was not dominated by any one advertiser, but Bank F was the leader with 24% share of spending, or $39.6M. Bank B and Bank A contributed over 20% each to the share of spending total.

Class Discussion/Questions

1. Why is it important for a company to review its past marketing efforts?

2. Why is it important for a company to continually monitor its competition?

3. Name a product category where there is a dominant leader. Discuss how that leader's innovations and marketing affect the other companies in the category.

Step 3: Target Market Effectors

This next step is perhaps the most critical component of a successful business review in providing valuable information for an actionable marketing plan. It is here that actual consumer purchase behavior is tracked, as well as awareness and attitudes which influence or determine that level of behavior. This data can be used to prepare marketing objectives, as well as awareness and attitude objectives throughout the marketing plan, particularly in the communications goals section where attitudes and awareness are linked directly to the marketing objectives, which in turn link directly to the sales objectives.

The chart on p. 76 of the text illustrates this. Accuracy here is essential to formulating those objectives, and the strategies for achieving them, in the rest of the plan. In some cases, the authors have prepared marketing plans based almost entirely on the information categorized in step 3.

Step 3 is based on the concept of the hierarchy of effects -- that a customer base (a subsection of the overall target market, characterized by repeat purchase behavior), is developed through a series of subsequent "effectors" among the target market, with each effector having an impact on the next. Repeat purchase follows initial trial, which results from positive attitudes about the product, which can only be achieved with a reasonable level of awareness among the target. Each subsequent effector results in a subsequently smaller subsection of the target market -- a certain percent of the target will be aware of the product or brand, a percent of those aware will form positive attitudes, a portion of whom will try the product, and finally a percentage of those who try will remain customers and continue to purchase.

The first task within this step is to fully identify the target market. Subsequent tasks review each of the effectors, with the intent of capturing for the business review the current status of the target for the students' product, in terms of awareness, attribute importance and relative perceived performance among the competitors, and current purchase and repurchase rates.

It will be easy for students to get bogged down in the numbers and details of each of these sections. Therefore, it will be useful for the instructor to continually refer to the overall target market and effectors, and how each task fits into the whole. Prepare an overhead or a large display board with a drawing similar to the chart on the bottom of page 74, illustrating the target market and effectors concept. Refer to this chart often, as you pass from one section to the next in working through the tasks. (A large sample is included on the next page for you to either copy onto an overhead or to blow up onto a large display board.)

Task 1: Review of Consumer and Business-to-Business Target Market Segments (pp. 75–93)

Target market definition is the most important step in preparing a business review. Effective marketing is impossible without a thorough understanding of your current and potential customer base. The more the customer can be understood, the better the marketer is able to fulfill the customer's needs. The emphasis of this task is to provide students with a format that sorts current and potential customers into segments. Segmenting allows customers to be grouped according to demographic, product usage, and purchasing characteristics. This allows for the analysis of which customer group is currently most profitable and which consumer group has the most potential.

This section provides a format which defined the profile of the <u>current category consumer</u> as compared to the <u>company's current consumer</u>. This allows the marketer to determine if the company's customer is different from the general product category consumer. The similarities and differences will be important when determining future marketing strategies. A company may find that its product is consumed by a far older population than the general product category's consumer. This important information can be used in the marketing plan to further target this older age segment or to develop plans to attract more of the younger, mainstream consumers.

Target Market and Effectors

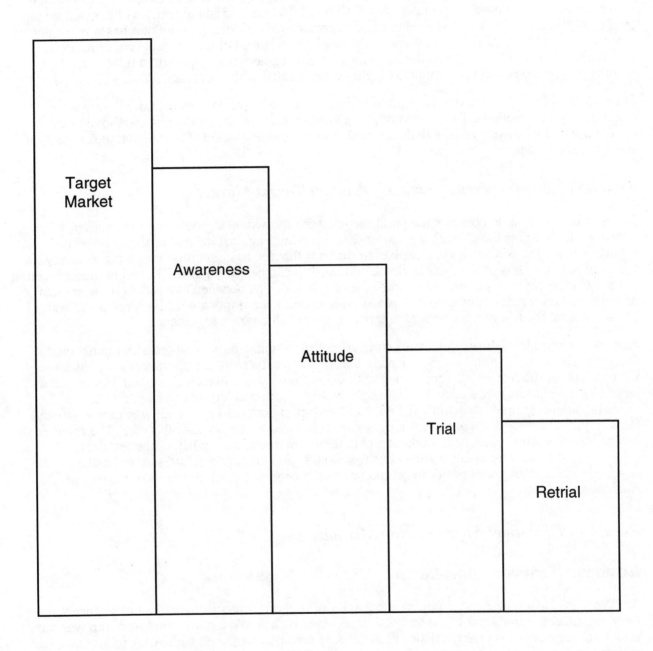

Volume and Concentration

It is important that students understand the basic concepts of volume and concentration, and how they help define the target market, and characterize individual segments within the target market, for their product or service. Volume refers to the sheer amount, or percent of total, of product consumed or purchased by a particular segment. Concentration refers to the percent of the particular segment who consume or purchase the product. (See Exhibits 2.14 and 2.15 in the text.) As the example on pp. 76–77 illustrates, 18 to 24 year olds might represent 15% of total product purchases in a category (volume), while 80% of all 18 to 24 year olds may be purchasers of the product (concentration). From this, you might suggest that the 18 to 24 year old segment may represent a relatively small volume of purchases, but the segment is highly concentrated with purchasers.

The benefits of this information is that a high concentration of purchasers is easier to target for a more efficient marketing effort. For example, a manufacturer of the product in the above example could target 18 to 24 year olds with direct mail, could provide products tailored to that segment, or specific promotions.

National Category versus Company/Product Target Market

Just as it is important to compare the purchase levels of individual segments to one another, it is important to compare those levels for the students' products against the rest of their respective product categories. Make sure you explain to students that the basic premise of the business review is to compare two sets of numbers so that a relationship can be established. The target market section of the business review is a prime example of how relationships between two sets of numbers can help the marketer reach conclusions. Discuss with students the implications, both good and bad, of variation from the rest of the category in terms of a product's target segments.

Here is an example of the usefulness of comparing the company target market with the national category. An off-price retail chain located in the Midwest sells suits and sport coats at a discount. Comparison of the retailer's target market with the national target market demographics of suit and sport coat purchasers revealed that Pells' target was far more blue-collar oriented. Further investigation determined that while the total suit and sport coat market overall was very small and shrinking, the blue-collar worker was a light-user compared to the white-collar user. The focus of the business review and subsequent marketing plan then centered around whether the retailer could afford to target this very small segment of the suit and sport coat market and stay in business. The firm eventually changed its positioning, and targeted businessmen, changing its name to Businessmenswear.

Review of Consumer Segmentation Methods

Customer Tenure Segmentation

Are there any differences in the purchase behavior of longer-term customers than more recent ones for your students' products? In the authors' experience with AAA, tenure of membership was an important segmentation characteristic. Those people who had remained with AAA more than five years tended to use more service and remain loyal AAA members, while earlier members tended not to renew as frequently nor did they use as many services. Discuss this example with the students, and provide other examples of situations where customer tenure can be a source of segmentation.

Demographic Segmentation (Description and Size)

Demographics describe the target market. Demographics for category users can be found in sources such as SMRB (Simmons Market Research Bureau) and Fairchild Fact Files or in trade magazine research studies. Demographics of customers come from company research. Make sure that students understand how to use these sources. Below is a test that will help make sure the students understand how the SRMB columns work. Have them provide you with the information to complete the blanks.

Total Female Head of Households

	Total U.S (000)	A (000)	B %	C %	D Index
Age	74,975	B____	100	85.7	100
18-24	A____	7,471	11.6	79.9	F____
25-34	17,130	C____	22.2	E____	97
35-44	12,512	11,066	17.2	88.4	103
45-54	11,866	10,678	16.6	90.0	105
55-64	10,905	9,698	D____	88.9	104
65+	13,214	11,052	17.2	83.6	98

Heavy User

		12,232	100	16.3	100
18-24	G____	973	8.0	10.4	64
25-34	17,130	2,268	18.5	13.2	81
35-44	12,512	2,919	23.9	23.3	143
45-54	11,866	2,305	18.6	19.4	119
55-64	10,905	1,978	16.2	18.1	111
65+	13,214	1,790	14.6	13.5	83

Answers

A: 9,348 (Subtract row of numbers under 74,975 from 74,975)

B: 64,266 (64,266 ÷ 74,975 = 85.7. Or 85.7 x 74,975 = 64,266)

C: 14,301 (Subtract column under 64,266 from 64,266. Or take 22.2% of 64,266—allow for rounding)

D: 15.09 (Take 9,698 and divide by 64,266)

E: 83.49 (Take 14,301 and divide by 17,130)

F: 93.23 (Take 79.9 and divide by 85.7)

G: 9,348 (Same as A)

Product Use

For some products, demographics aren't as demonstrative in product purchase or use. Many times purchasers with similar demographics purchase the product for different reasons. This offers the opportunity to segment consumers based upon usage of the product. Listed below are two examples of products with users who use the product for different reasons. Use these examples in class to have students discuss how you would market differently to the different groups for each product:

— Mercedes-Benz: high-priced luxury cars versus mass appeal family cars. Purchasers buy the Mercedes Benz for quality and to make a statement about their life-style and accomplishments.

— Premium Beers: targets upscale consumers who drink fewer beers and consume beer as much or more at restaurants than at home. Premium beer drinkers purchase the product in a social setting making a statement about themselves with the beer they drink.

Psychographic/Lifestyle Segmentation

Just as demographics describe members of a market segment, a population can also be segmented by virtue of their personality traits, lifestyle characteristics, attitudes and beliefs. Discuss each of the four major lifestyle systems described in the text. It may be useful to pick up a book on one of the four methods, and have students put themselves into categories based on the particular lifestyle system.

Attribute Segmentation

Certain product category purchasers can be defined by a particular attribute they seek from the category. Discuss the examples provided in the text, and ask students if any of their assigned products share this characteristic.

Heavy User Segmentation

Most product categories have a group of heavy users—consumers who purchase or use the product at far greater rates than that of the average consumer. According to our definition, a category has a meaningful heavy-user segment if approximately one third or less of the consumers account for approximately two thirds or more of the purchases.

This section helps students determine if a heavy-user category exists and in comparing the heavy user profile to the profile of the company they are studying (see Exhibits 2.19 and 2.20 plus utilize Exhibit 2.16 with heavy-user data). A company which does not attract the heavy user needs to utilize different marketing strategies than the company who attracts the heavy user.

— Has a more narrowly defined target market.

— Need to capture a larger market share of non-heavy user target market than would be necessary if the company was targeting the heavy user.

— Often, a company targeting a non-heavy user segment is providing product attributes that vary from the heavy user needs and wants and thus are slightly different than the typical category purchaser.

Examples of firms targeting a consumer profile which is different from the heavy user in their category follow. You might discuss how marketing differs for these companies versus the typical category marketer.

— Men's Shoe Stores: The heavy user in the shoe category is the female with children. Men account for a small percentage of the shoe purchases, yet there are stores dedicated to the male shoe purchaser.

— Imported Beer: The vast majority of beer consumed is in the middle price range. However, imported beer, and more recently "micro" beer, is more expensive and consumed in restaurants as well as in the home, and is very popular among upscale business people and college students.

Class Discussion/Questions

1. Why is it important to compare a company's demographics to the product category's demographics? What type of information can be determined from this comparison?

2. Why are demographics alone not enough? What else does a marketer need to know about the target market?

3. Why is the heavy user group important to the marketer? Does it ever pay to ignore this group?

4. What is the difference between a demographic volume measure and concentration measure? How does a marketer use both of these measures?

Review of Business-to-Business Segmentation Methods

Business-to-business firms typically have far fewer potential customers than consumer companies. In addition, each business-to-business customer usually generates larger sales than does the typical consumer customer. As with consumer target markets, it is important that students understand how to develop a business-to-business segmenting methodology so that they can determine which type of business is most profitable and has the most potential. (Note: this is an important step if your groups are involved with either business-to-business firm or if they are focusing on a package goods firm which has both a consumer target market and a business-to-business target.)

This step has two main sections:

1. Target market segmentation and Standard Industrial Classification (SIC) categories. This section should be very easy for students to understand. It involves using the charts that correspond to Appendix B to determine the number of potential customers and the penetration of the company against each customer group. The customers and potential customers are grouped by SICs. SICs are explain on page 89 of the text. Reproduce for students the following SIC classifications and groupings to discuss in class.

2. Other methods of segmenting are discussed on pages 91–92. This section briefly covers additional ways to segment business-to-business companies. The methods discussed include dollar size; employee size; heavy usage rates; product application/use; organizational structure; new versus repeat buyer; geographic location; and decision makers and influencers.

Four-digit SIC Totals

Agriculture, Forestry, and Fishing — 336,950

SIC Numbers 0100-0999

SIC	Description	Count
01	Agricultural Production-Crops	160,047
0111	Wheat Farm	19,498
0112	Rice Farm	2,280
0115	Corn Farm	35,561
0116	Soybean Farm	2,991
0119	Cash Grains, NEC	6,938
0131	Cotton Farm	6,084
0132	Tobacco Farm	732
0133	Sugarcane & Sugar Beet Farm	511
0134	Irish Potato Farm	1,308
0139	Field Crops Exc Cash, NEC	2,670
0161	Vegetable & Melon Farm	3,974
0171	Berry Crop Farm	847
0172	Grape Vineyard	1,379
0173	Tree Nut Grove	707
0174	Citrus Fruit Grove	1,369
0175	Deciduous Tree Fruit Orchard	3,822
0179	Fruit & Tree Nut, NEC	348
0181	Grow Flowers/Nursery Products	12,551
0182	Food Crops (Under Cover)	979
0191	General Farms	55,498
02	Agricultural Production-Livestock	59,947
0211	Beef Cattle Feedlots	2,800
0212	Beef Cattle, Exc Feedlots	17,427
0213	Hogs	3,939
0214	Sheep & Goats	674
0219	Livestock Exc Dairy/Poultry	839
0241	Dairy Farm	12,963
0251	Raising Cooking Chickens	979
0252	Chicken Eggs	1,365
0253	Turkeys & Turkey Eggs	649
0254	Poultry Hatcheries	759
0259	Poultry & Eggs, NEC	227
0271	Fur-Bearing Animal Farms	639
0272	Horses & Other Equines	2,602
0273	Animal Aquaculture	611
0279	Animal Specialties, NEC	2,396
0291	Livestock & Animal Farms	11,078
07	Agricultural Services	110,233
0711	Soil Preparation Svcs	1,375
0721	Crop Planting & Cultivating	4,046
0722	Crop Machine Harvesting Svcs	1,637
0723	Crops Preparation Exc Cot Gin	2,909
0724	Cotton Ginning	1,576
0741	Livestock Veterinary Svc	2,250
0742	Veterinary Svcs, Animals	20,921
0751	Livestock Svc Exc Veterinary	2,310
0752	Animal Svcs Exc Veterinary	13,532
0761	Farm Labor Contractors	356
0762	Farm Mgt Svcs	1,072
0781	Landscape Plan/Consult	11,791
0782	Lawn & Garden Svcs	38,899
0783	Ornamental Shrub & Tree Svcs	7,559
08	Forestry	4,035
0811	Timber Tracts	1,540
0831	Forest Nurseries & Products	348
0851	Forestry Svcs	2,147
09	Fishing, Hunting, and Trapping	2,688
0912	Finfish	948
0913	Shellfish	920
0919	Misc Marine Products	51
0921	Fish Hatchery & Preserve	516
0971	Hunt/Trap/Propagation	253

Mining — 51,040

SIC Numbers 1000-1499

SIC	Description	Count
10	Metal Mining	1,884
1011	Iron Ores	94
1021	Copper Ores	90
1031	Lead & Zinc Ores	71
1041	Gold Ores	712
1044	Silver Ores	114
1061	Ferroalloy Ores Exc Vanadium	44
1081	Metal Mining Services	519
1094	Uranium-Radium-Vanadium	155
1099	Misc Metal Ores, NEC	85
12	Coal Mining	5,734
1221	Bit/Lignite Surface Mining	3,330
1222	Bit Coal Underground Mining	803
1231	Anthracite Mining	344
1241	Coal Mining Svcs	1,257
13	Oil and Gas Extraction	37,837
1311	Crude Petroleum & Nat Gas	14,926
1321	Produce Natural Gas Liquids	234
1381	Drilling Oil & Gas Wells	4,642
1382	Oil/Gas Field Exploration Svc	5,555
1389	Oil/Gas Field Svcs, NEC	12,480
14	Nonmetallic Minerals, except Fuels	5,585
1411	Dimension Stone	437
1422	Crushed/Broken Limestone	990
1423	Crushed/Broken Granite	96
1429	Crushed/Broken Stone, NEC	372
1442	Construction Sand & Gravel	2,364
1446	Industrial Sand	189
1455	Kaolin & Ball Clay	63
1459	Clay Refractory Minerals, NEC	157
1474	Potash/Soda/Borate Minerals	31
1475	Phosphate Rock	36
1479	Chemical Mineral Mining, NEC	125
1481	Nonmetal Minerals Exc Fuels	228
1499	Misc Nonmetals Exc Fuels	497

Construction — 872,259

SIC Numbers 1500-1799

SIC	Description	Count
15	General Building Contractors	311,220
1521	General House Contractors	214,356
1522	Residential Bldgs exc houses	14,559
1531	Operative Builders	21,601
1541	Industrial Bldg/Warehse	11,761
1542	Nonresidential Bldgs exc ind.	48,943
16	Heavy Construction, except Building	45,932
1611	Road Construct Exc El Hways	16,294
1622	Bridge/Tunnel/El Hway Const	1,660
1623	Utility/Pwr Line Construction	13,635
1629	Heavy Construction, NEC	14,343
17	Special Trade Contractors	515,107
1711	Plumbing, Heating & A/C	125,046
1721	Painting & Paper Hanging	45,349
1731	Electrical Work	84,476
1741	Masonry/Stone Set/Other Work	22,659
1742	Plaster/Wall/Insulation Work	24,691
1743	Tile, Marble, Mosaic Work	8,108
1751	Carpentry Work	25,243
1752	Floor Work, NEC	13,879
1761	Roof/Siding/Sheet Metal Work	38,707
1771	Concrete Work	26,760
1781	Water Well Drilling	7,218
1791	Erect Structural Steel	4,955
1793	Glass & Glazing Work	7,026
1794	Excavation Work	38,415
1795	Wrecking & Demolition Work	1,886
1796	Install/Erect Bldg Equip, NEC	3,013
1799	Special Trade Contractors, NEC	37,676

All counts are primary SICs only

Class Discussion/Questions

1. Why is it important to compare a company's demographics/SIC to the product category demographics/SICs? What type of information can be determined from this comparison?

2. What is the difference between a demographic volume measure and concentration measure? How does a marketer use both of these measures?

3. Why are demographics alone not enough? What else does a marketer need to know about the target market?

4. Why is the heavy user group important to the marketer? Does it ever pay to ignore this group?

5. What is an SIC code? How does the business-to-business marketer use SIC codes?

6. Why is segmenting important for the business-to-business marketer? How is segmenting accomplished? Discuss the two-step process outlined in the text.

Task 2: Product Awareness and Attributes (pp. 93–98)

This step is broken into three sections: product awareness; product attributes; and product life cycle.

Awareness

There are three measures of awareness:

— First Mention Unaided (Top-of-Mind): This is the most indicative of market share. Usually the first company or brand mentioned when consumers are asked to list companies or products is the one the consumer is most likely to shop or purchase.

— Total Unaided: Companies or brands that are listed without the researcher aiding the consumer by mentioning names of firms or brands, are considered in the "evoke set" of the consumer. For example, if the consumer mentions three companies or brands, the first one mentioned (first mention) will most likely get the most business. However, the other two are either secondary brands or companies, or are considered when making a purchase.

In connection with the unaided score, it is important to look at the brand loyalty of the category. If a category is non-brand loyal, first mention is not as significant. Consumers shop multiple brands or companies so the total unaided score becomes all the most significant.

— Total Aided Awareness: This is the combined awareness score when the researcher goes beyond unaided and prompts the consumer with "Have you heard of X, Y, and Z companies or brands?" We don't put much emphasis on this awareness measure. However, it does serve a purpose and that is as a base measure. If the firm has a low competitive aided awareness figure, the marketing efforts have a long way to go—the product or company has to focus first on building awareness as it is not even in the playing field.

Attributes

The key here is to make certain the students understand the importance of the questions on page 96. Most important is for the marketers to have an idea of the most important rated attributes and how their company or product rates on those attributes relative to the competition.

This section ties in directly to the work students will be doing on positioning later in the class. You might point this out so they keep remembering there is a reason for developing this fairly extensive marketing database.

The first two sections, awareness and attributes, are critical for students yet if the class structure is one of application or case study, will be the most difficult to gather data. In most businesses this type of data is obtained through primary research studies. Attributes are discussed on pp. 95 and 96 of the text. Also refer to the sample research questionnaires at the end of Chapter 1 if the students are inclined to develop primary research or if you wish to further discuss ways to gather this type of information during class.

Life Cycle

This section does not require primary research. We suggest you take students through the examples in the text, starting on pages 97–98. Use the following to aid class discussion.

Introduction: New product planning receives more attention than most other areas of marketing. It is often seen as the lifeblood of most companies. In most industries, competitive pressures require constant improvement or innovation of products in order to increase or even maintain market share. While it is impossible to provide an exact figure, new products or extensions and improvements on old products can be attributable to over half of the sales gains for many companies. Sales gains for consumer companies, such as cosmetics and children's toys are even higher. But new product development is expensive—on average, only one or two new products out of 10 survive.

Discuss the many factors that influence the acceptance of a new product in the marketplace. Business-to-business firms often have a longer introductory period than consumer firms because there are typically more people involved in the purchase decision process. However, once integrated into the business channels, the products become ingrained and often stay for a long time. The opposite holds true for consumer items, particularly trendy fashion items that tend to catch on quickly and then fade away. In summary, the following is a list of factors you might discuss with students that affect the length of the introductory stage of a new product and lead to a greater propensity for risk on the part of the company introducing the product:

— The more decision makers in the purchase decision (business-to-business buying groups), the longer the introductory stage.

— The more complex the product and the more education that the consumer needs before understanding the product's benefits, the longer the introductory stage.

— Fashion of youth orientation typically results in a faster introduction stage.

— Typically, the more the product costs, the longer it takes to pass through the introductory stage.

— The more noticeable the purchase (and the greater the degree of ego involvement with the purchase), the longer it will take for consumers to test the product and the longer it will take for the product to become mainstream.

Examples of products in the introductory stage include: cell phones; snow boards; and fashion apparel.

Growth: Oftentimes during the growth stage of the product life cycle, product innovation occurs. It is important that the students realize that product innovation is as important as new product development. Extension of product use forces a marketing organization to react to the competitive environment. The best product extension examples are in the area of foods and package goods. How many products can your students think of that started out in one flavor or one size and then extended into multiple flavors or sizes to segment and take advantage of consumer demand?

— Jello (colors, pudding pops, etc.)

— 3M scotch tape in different sizes and colors and for different purposes (book binding tape, gift wrapping tape, tape to write on, Post-it-notes, etc.)

— Toothpaste (regular, gel, tartar control, etc.)

Maturity: The text does a good job of describing the maturity stage in terms of the marketing environment. However, it does not cover the real decision issues during this stage in terms of deciding to eliminate or stop spending money against a product. When this happens, spending against the product is substantially reduced in an effort to gain as much profits as possible. This of course is a short-term strategy in that no long-term consumer franchise is being built, only short-term profit taking. In the end, the decision may be to kill the product all together. In marketing literature, much is written about new product introductions and development—not much is written about the decision-making process for deleting a product from the product line.

The industry that is probably best a cutting the losses of unprofitable products is the mail order business. We could all stand to learn from their examples. Catalogers spend a great deal of time determining exactly how much each square inch of any given catalog costs in terms of product, distribution, and advertising costs. If a product is not carrying its weight and is not generating profits, it is very quickly eliminated from the product mix and replaced with a product that will generate more profits than it costs to carry it in the catalog.

A product in the mature stage of the product life cycle should be targeted for elimination if the following combination of factors are present:

— The product's sales trend has been declining faster than other products in your company's mix.

— The product category's sales trends nationally have been declining.

— Substitute products with competitive advantages such as cheaper price or more favorable attributes are available.

— The company's product and the product category nationally has experienced a decline in price.

— The company's product has incurred increased expenses, lower margins, or decreased profits.

— In business-to-business markets, there is a sales decline in the products that your product is dependent upon for ultimate sales. For example, if you sell to an OEM and the product the OEM manufacturers has experienced a decline in sales, you might consider focusing attention away from this product line.

Class Discussion/Questions

1. What is the difference between first mention top -of-mind awareness, total unaided awareness, and total aided awareness? Which one is a better indicator of market share?

2. How do marketers use awareness data in helping them to develop marketing strategy? (A product that has high dominant awareness will typically dominate in market share. Low awareness levels lead to marketing programs aimed at creating awareness of the product and reviewing media strategies to make certain the advertising is being placed in the most optimum mediums, at the optimum media weight, to most effectively reach and motivate the target market to action. Falling awareness levels in established high awareness markets often call for increased review of competitive activity, a change or improvement in product attributes, or more media weight and special marketing programs to regain lost awareness and reestablish the product in the consumers' minds. Finally, tracking awareness levels allows a marketer to monitor the overall success of the company's marketing effort, as increased awareness usually leads to increased behavior or market share.)

3. How do marketers use product attribute information? What attributes are most important to score well on in consumer surveys?

4. What can be done to stop the product life cycle and products from reaching maturity and decline? Name some examples of products that have stayed innovative and have continued to create additional demand for the product category and themselves.

Task 3: Trial and Retrial Behavior (pp. 98–104)

Students should analyze the trial and retrial behavior of the target market to further determine where, how, and why consumers are purchasing the company's product. Buying habit information can provide invaluable insight into the target market and provide impact for marketing decisions. These decisions revolve around either trying to change current consumption patterns (which is most difficult) or recognizing the patterns and modifying the product, or the way in which the product is sold to better meet the needs of the target market.

Task 3 is divided into three major sections: 1.) trial behavior, including buying habits, purchase rates of the product category and your company's product by geographic markets, and trading areas; 2.) retrial behavior, including brand loyalty; and 3.) trial to retrial ratio.

Trial Behavior

Buying Habits

This section can be handled by discussing the questions to be addressed section on page 99 and reviewing the worksheet in Appendix B.

One additional exercise we have found helpful in illustrating this section is to ask students about the buying habits of a potential employer interviewing students. Ask the students to answer the questions on page 99 in the context of the employer being the target market of the students. Then ask the students to relate the answers to developing potential job hunting strategies. This exercise always seems to get a spirited response and approaches the topic in a memorable way from the students' perspective.

Purchase Rates

The first section demonstrates how to use two index relationships, CDI and BDI. The text contains the formulas and explanations of both of these terms. You may wish to use the following exercise to help explain the two terms and to make the students familiar with how to use the indexes.

DMA	% Total U.S. Hhds	% Product Consumed Nat'l	% Company Target Market	% Company Business	CDI	BDI
Philadelphia	2.9	3.9	12	10	135	83
Detroit	1.9	2.1	12	9	111	75
Denver	1.1	0.7	10	12	64	120
Columbus, OH	0.7	1.1	10	13	157	130
Dayton	0.5	0.5	7	8	100	114
Tulsa	0.5	0.7	6	10	140	167
Toledo	0.4	0.3	5	5	75	100
Pittsburgh	1.3	1.8	13	20	138	154
Minneapolis	1.4	1.3	15	13	93	87

The following observations can be made about the above chart. The high BDI markets are successful markets for the company being studied. These markets should receive first priority. Due to penetration/distribution, a weaker competitive set, and/or effective marketing—sales have been healthy. However, the next step is to review the CDI or market potential to make decisions as to

66

whether additional markets should receive incremental spending, perhaps even slightly reducing the spending in markets with strong BDIs but weak CDIs in favor of markets with strong CDIs and lower BDIs (those that show market potential beyond current performance).

— Philadelphia, Detroit, Columbus, Tulsa, and Pittsburgh are all markets which do well from a national category standpoint.

— Philadelphia and Detroit should receive priority attention. They have a high CDI but a low BDI. This means that while category purchases are above average for the market (high CDI) the company is doing relatively poorly compared to other company markets (low BDI). The first place to check is penetration. Philadelphia and Detroit are very large markets and if the markets are not adequately penetrated with stores or they do not have enough distribution/shelf space, the BDIs will be low (large percent of system households, small percent of system sales). After the penetration has been studied, other variables such as competition, advertising spending, and product mix should be analyzed. If primary research exist, an analysis should be done to see what are the most important consumer product attributes and how the company ranks relative to the competition on those attributes.

— A market like Denver is penetrated and perhaps even over penetrated. It is a mature market. The BDI is substantially higher than the average BDI and there is an inverse relationship between the CDI and BDI (high BDI and low CDI). A market like Denver might see slightly reduced spending in favor of markets with more potential (higher CDI).

Trading Areas

Trading area information is typically obtained through in-store surveys. At this point you might discuss with your students the uses of trading area information and how it might later be used in developing the marketing plan.

Zip Codes	Trading Area % Customers	Distance from Store for Retailers/ Distance Travel for Purchase of Consumer Goods
53704	58	2 miles
53705	20	4 miles
55715	12	6 miles
55742	8	10 miles
55775	2	15 miles

Question: What implications would the above trading area data have from a strategic standpoint?

Discussion Starter: A company might choose to utilize very targeted media against the zip codes that account for 70% of the customers. Or the decision may be made to broaden the geographic target market by obtaining a larger number of purchases from a greater distance. This could be done through utilizing alternative, localized media or direct mail. A decision may be made to increase penetration in areas with a low percentage of purchasers. Finally, if you know that your product typically has a fairly large trading area, you may choose to analyze the trading areas in terms of demographics, life-style and purchase patterns to determine if there is some consistent reason why some zip code areas produce more customers than others. This information will be useful in future targeting and in developing marketing programs.

Brand Loyalty

It is important for the students to realize that not all product categories have the same level of brand loyalty. Categories where price is more important than product, quality, and service attributes have lesser degrees of brand loyalty. Product categories where product, quality, and service factors are more important than price have larger degrees of brand loyalty. In addition, the greater the product's risk or price (the chance that the consumer will make a poor purchase decision) and the greater the consumer's ego involvement with the product, the greater the brand loyalty.

We suggest that you discuss the five reasons brand loyalty is analyzed on page 103 and review Exhibit 2.26 on page 103 which demonstrates how to calculate brand loyalty. The following may help you.

— Different companies exhibit different degrees of consumer loyalty. For example, a retailer of shoes has much less store loyalty than a retailer of skis. This is because of the nature of the product the two different retailers sell. Shoes require very little sales service, the customer is an expert in what he or she needs. However with skis, the customer needs the expertise of the store personnel to help fit boots and make the correct purchase decision in what is a fairly technical decision. Thus ski retailers will have a more store loyal customer base than will the shoe retailer.

In the consumer package goods area, manufacturers spend a great deal of money to create a brand loyal consumer base. Brand loyalty can be found in products in which the manufacturer has successfully created product differences (more raisins in the bran flakes, softer tissues for your nose) or where the brand name has become associated with a quality product or differentiated product attribute.

— A product or company with low brand loyalty (many retail stores, manufacturers of generic products) has to rely on promotion to a greater degree than pure advertising. The objective is to continually provide the consumer with a reason to purchase.

— A company with low brand or store loyalty typically has to spend more money on promotion, provide customers stronger promotional offers, and usually has to take less margin dollars in the form of a lower pricing structure in order to attract customers. Have students provide you with examples of the above.

— A category with low brand or store loyalty will be easier to steal market share than one with a high degree of brand loyalty. In addition, in a category with high brand loyalty, the media expenditures required to steal market share from a specific competitor(s) are often higher due to the satisfaction level of the consumers.

— In categories where there is a high degree of brand loyalty, a product innovation or improvement is often needed to effectively compete for increased market share.

Trial to Retrial Ratio

This section can be discussed through review of the text and questions to be addressed portion of the chapter. You may wish to use the following as a discussion-starter:

— Low trial: Probably either low awareness problems or poor attitude ratings on key category attributes.

— Low retrial: Product performance problems in terms of attribute ratings.

— Low overall trial but strong retrial from those who have tried: The product is very well received once tried. The problem could be a small target market, limitedawareness, or poor perceptions of the product.

Class Discussion/Questions

1. If a market has a high CDI and a low BDI, what are the implications?

2. What determines a company's trading area? (The type of product . . . specifically items with higher price tags and ego-involved products have large trading areas and basic shopping goods have a relatively small trading area.)

3. Name products with high-brand loyalty (beer, peanut butter) and low-brand loyalty (shoe stores, pens, socks, generic goods). How does a marketer market differently for a low-brand loyalty product versus a high-brand loyalty product?

4. If your product has a low overall trial but high retrial, what are the marketing implications?

Business Review Writing Style (pp. 104–105)

Make sure the students realize the importance of writing objective, concise statements summarizing their findings. The examples on page 72 demonstrate how a summary statement is followed by the data supporting that statement. Insist that the students write in a business style. Make sure they do not write as if developing a novel. Remind them that the most valuable commodity in business is time. Long does not get read.

Review the Dos and Don'ts at the end of the chapter. Discuss questions at this time before moving into the problems and opportunities and plan sections of the book.

CHAPTER 3

PROBLEMS AND OPPORTUNITIES

Chapter Objectives

1. Demonstrate how to identify problems and opportunities from the material the students developed in the business review.

2. Teach how to write succinct, actionable problems and opportunities in a format that allows an organized transition into writing the marketing plan.

Teaching Suggestions

1. This is a section of the overall marketing document that students in an applications course often have to rewrite, at least once. The tendency is to breathe a sigh of relief after completing the business review. Therefore, not enough time is put in developing problems and opportunities from the data collected. Always develop as a many meaningful problems and opportunities as possible. Stress that it's important to go in with the goal of developing too many, reducing, and summarizing at a later time.

2. One disadvantage is that the students have never done this before. Therefore, we recommend that some class time be used to review the problems and opportunities examples in the text. This helps the students get a feel for what is expected and how to write the statements.

3. If the course is not an applications course, provide case examples, and ask the students to prepare problems and opportunities based on the case situations.

4. Make sure that students stick to writing objective statements. This is not the place for strategy.

5. Make sure students include the obvious. They often try to make this too difficult. For example, a company might have been losing market share, or has a low awareness rating, or has had a new strong competitor enter the marketplace, or is suffering financial problems. All of these, while basic problems, are key factors in determining marketing objectives and strategies. Include the obvious. These are often the things that will account for the major focus of the plan.

Class Discussion/Questions

1. Have each student provide an example of key problems or opportunities they have found to-date in working on the business review or from an industry example they are familiar with. See how many students can list without using much thought. Make sure that they are including problems and opportunities from each of the business review steps.

2. How do you determine whether the finding is a problem or opportunity? (See page 110.)

3. Review the Dos and Don'ts at the end of the chapter.

CHAPTER 4

SALES OBJECTIVES

Chapter Objectives

1. Review the definition and importance of sales objectives.

2. Review properties of sales objectives and that they must relate in terms of being time specific, quantifiable, and profit related.

3. Review the quantitative and qualitative factors to be considered in setting sales objectives.

4. Discuss the three-step process of setting sales objectives.

    a. Set quantitative objectives

       — Macro: Outside/marketed generated

       — Micro: Inside/company generated

       — Expenses plus: Budget based

    b. Reconcile the quantitatively generated sales objectives into one dollar objective and unit objective for each of the next three years.

    c. Qualitatively adjust the quantitative sales objective(s) arrived at through reconciliation.

5. Discuss other potential methods of setting sales objectives.

6. Review various reasons for eventual revision of "going-in" sales objectives in developing a marketing plan.

Teaching Suggestions

1. While the methodology for setting sales objectives is relatively straightforward, it is a good idea to ask various students in the class to accurately explain the macro, micro, and budget-based methods and discuss any questions or problems regarding their application.

2. Often, the biggest problem students experience with setting sales objectives is the generation of raw numbers for each macro approach in order to apply the methodology. If you are following the campaigns format, student teams will have to do a thorough search of the available market and company data in order to generate the raw numbers. To help them in the process, ask the client to provide students with as much of the raw data as possible during their class presentation, including, for example, the data that pertains to the company's past sales along with the business performance data in terms of expense and margin information ad resulting bottom-line profits.

3. Because of the difficulty in generating raw data, suggest that students be creative in filling the data voids through simulation of information for competitive products. For example, students might review the sales data of competitive products and use an interpolation of these numbers as the basis for the three-step process. This approach is particularly helpful if the product is a new one with no company product sales history. For example, if the competition's product garnered a two-share its first year, and a three- and four-share its second and third, respectively, a similar scenario could be projected for their new product being introduced. Most importantly for this type of approach and the final sales profit objectives, a rationale should be included in the interim report.

4. Another approach to generating sales objectives, particularly if the product being introduced represents a new product category such as the introduction of the first VCR or soft soap, is to review the potential target market and work backward to a sales objective number. An example for a package goods product follows:

Potential target market consumers (Defined by demography, geography, usage, etc.)	2,500M
Expected trial rate	4%
Initial trial units	100M
% making repeat purchase	40%
Repeat purchases	40M
Number of repeat purchases	5
Repeat units	200M
Initial trial units	100M
Units sold nationally	300M
Cases (12 units per case)	25M
Gross Sales (@ $10.74/case)	$268.5M

Obviously critical to this type of target market generated sales objectives are the initial estimates of the target market potential, trial, and repeat projections. Unless based on a related or closely simulated historical data, sales objectives generated in this manner are highly speculative and thus can be highly inaccurate. It is best to use the target market approach only when data for the other methods of sales forecasting do not exist or in conjunction with one or all of the other methods discussed in the text.

5. In most cases the client will not have the necessary information for the application of the bottom-up approach of the "micro-company" based method. Accordingly, the sales estimates generated from the top approach will represent the micro-generated sales estimate.

6. In some cases, sales objectives are provided by the client, often set by the company's management. The sales objectives portion of the plan will then illustrate what is required of each customer segment, each store, each geographic area, or some other appropriate segment, through the micro and macro approaches, to achieve the dictated sales goals.

7. Make sure that once sales objectives have been determined, corresponding profit goals are also established by taking into consideration the company's performance in terms of margins and expenses.

8. Make sure that students understand that going-in sales and profit objectives will most likely be revised as the marketing plan is prepared. Revisions might be dependent on whether national, regional, or local plans are developed. Consideration of this type will add or limit product sales for the pan. And as mentioned in the text, original sales objectives are usually reviewed based on the potential of the target market purchasing the product and the cost of executing the marketing

plan in a competitive environment. This is especially important for students of an applications course who will feel frustrated by this constant changing, and making the necessary revisions.

9. It is recommended that students follow the marketing plan format provided in Appendix C when preparing written sales objectives (and all other marketing plan components) in order for the necessary information to be included in an efficient, meaningful, and comprehensive form. Sales objectives, as well as all the other objectives and strategies throughout the marketing plan, should be the first data presented for each respective segment of the marketing plan. The rationale and back-up calculations that lead to the objectives and strategies should follow.

10. Make sure that students' understand that sales objectives for manufacturers represent the company's sales to its immediate customer not the retailer's sales to the final purchaser or user.

Class Discussion/Questions

1. Discuss the difference between quantitative and qualitative information.

2. Discuss the issue that generating sales objectives is <u>not</u> a science but a balanced approach with the combination of quantitative (hard data) and qualitative (soft data) information.

3. Ask students if they can think of other qualitative factors to be considered in setting sales objectives, other than those mentioned in the text. (For example, retail trade practices in pricing and merchandising the product.)

4. Why is it necessary to set more than sales dollar objectives?

5. Why is it wise to use more than one method in arriving at a sales objective?

6. Discuss how an product manager would reconcile (if considerably different) what the company or division management expects in terms of sales or profits versus what the product manager includes in his or her marketing plans.

CHAPTER 5

TARGET MARKET AND MARKETING OBJECTIVES

Chapter Objectives

1. Define the following:

   — target markets and segmentation

   — primary target

   — secondary target

   — influencer

   — marketing objective

2. Determine how to define the primary consumer and business-to-business target markets.

3. Determine how to define secondary consumer and business-to-business target markets.

4. Learn how to write succinct target market descriptors.

5. Understand how marketing objectives tie the target market to the sales objectives.

6. Make sure the students know how to develop marketing objectives.

Teaching Suggestions

1. The data developed in the Business Review under Step 3 should provide students with a quantitative description of target markets for a particular product category. Now students must use that information to make decisions as to the identity of the primary and secondary target markets.

   Sometimes the target market section in the business review is incomplete or there was not enough secondary information available to provide a quantitative database. If this is the case, have the students talk with the trade, media reps, retailers, or competitors in an attempt to answer the same questions posed in the business review section:

   — What are the demographics of the target market?

74

— What are the demographics of the target market that has the greatest volume of usage and the greatest concentration of users?

— What are the demographics of segments as defined by product usage and do they differ?

— Is there a heavy user?

2. Take the students step-by-step through the process of defining the primary target segment, as detailed in the text. Work with their assigned business or provide another example for the whole class to follow.

— Sales/Profits: Use the Product Sales Volume chart in Appendix C to lay out the products with the largest sales volume and/or growth. Focus on users and/or purchasers of these specific products.

— Segments: Begin by looking broadly at current customers and new potential customers for the product identified above. Break these groups into smaller segments by characteristics which determine purchase volume, such as demographics, product use, etc.

— Awareness: Review the awareness of your example company or its product/brand among the considered target segments.

— Attitudes: Review the attitudes about your example company or its product/brand held by the considered target segments.

— Decision Criteria: Finally, apply the criteria on page 145 to your considered segments to determine which to keep as your final target.

— Product Mix: Review the mix of products most consumed/purchased by your remaining segments.

— Demand Analysis: Calculate the total potential volume demanded by your chosen segments, based roughly on your example company's share applied to the specific segments you've selected (see pages 146–147). This step is important because these segments must provide enough potential purchases to achieve your sales objectives.

3. It is important for the students to define their target market not only by demographics and geography but also by usage. That's where the heavy-user calculation and volume measure starts students in the right direction. In addition to defining target markets by volume of purchases, consider defining target markets by size of purchases, frequency of purchases, and reasons for purchase (for example, price versus quality).

4. Discuss the process of segmenting in the business-to-business market. For many companies who target business, the methodology provided on pp. 148–149 is logical and relatively easy. Defining existing core customers, task 1, can be achieved by reviewing internal sales information, by customer segment (SIC, business size, geography, etc.) -- those segments with the largest sales volume, growth and longevity represent the core customers. The segment description that defines the core current customers becomes the basis for targeting prospects with high potential. This can be enhanced by interviewing the sales staff -- what types of companies are their best prospects, have the most potential, best "fit" their product or service offerings? Answers to these questions provide the basis of task 2. Finally, task 3 requires identifying the key decision-makers within the targeted organizations. In some cases, this may be an entire team of people, from vice-presidents to office staff.

5. Discuss the definition of marketing objectives by emphasizing the fact that marketing objectives "focus on affecting target market behavior." This provides an understanding of how a marketing objective differs from other communication objectives, such as advertising objectives and publicity objectives. It also helps explain how marketing objectives relate to the target market and sales objectives. The sales objectives define marketing and product goals while the target market is the generator to fulfill the sales goals. The marketing objectives describe how the target market has to be affected in order to achieve the sales goals. Once a student understands that a marketing objective affects target market behavior, then it is an easy next step to discuss that the target market can either be existing or new customers and that the objectives can focus on the following:

— From existing customers, the marketer can either retain current customers or increase purchases from current customers.

— From new customers the marketer can either increase trial of the product or store or obtain repeat usage of the product or store.

6. Review Exhibit 5.8 with the students. This chart helps to illustrate how marketing objectives form a quantifiable bridge between the target market and the plan strategies, providing the behavior required of each segment to achieve the sales objectives.

7. We suggest that you make Exhibit 5.9 on page 156 part of your class discussion. This rationale exercise seems to help cement in students' minds the idea of how a marketing objective affects consumer behavior in a way that ties directly back to sales.

8. All of the information required to calculate marketing objectives should be available in the business review. Review each of the primary marketing objectives with students, and suggest what information will help them quantify the specific objectives:

— Retention of customers: Base on historical retention rates for your company relative to the category or key competitors.

— Purchase rates: You're likely to want to increase this, so observe the historical rate for your firm and compare to the rest of the industry to set the objective. It would be unreasonable, for example, to expect to increase your customer's purchases from 6 to 8 times per year if the industry average is only 6.5. Also, the purchase rate is likely to be lower for new customers than for existing customers.

— Dollar volume per purchase: Again, you will probably want to increase the dollar per purchase, but compare your company's historical amounts to the industry. Some increase may be expected naturally if the company and/or industry have been trending up, and vice versa. Also, new customers are also likely to spend less per purchase than existing customers.

— Store visits or quotes: One additional behavior may be required to turn sales among retailers is store visits. An objective for this should be included in the Marketing Objectives. Similarly, certain firms, especially in business-to-business situations, often need to provide quotes before getting a customer. Historical information should be available in the business review for the ratio of store visits to purchases or the ratio of quotes to jobs to provide the basis for the objectives.

9. Often, companies do not have good information bases from which to capture data for calculating marketing objectives. In such cases, primary research can be used. Quantitative surveys can provide data on retention, purchase rates, store visits, dollars spent per visit/transaction, trial, etc.

Class Discussion/Questions

1. What is the difference between defining a target market and segmenting a target market?

2. Can the target market account for less than 30% – 50% of the consumption of the product and still be successful? Why or why not?

3. Have students provide target markets for companies you provide them. Provide groupings of two companies within the same product category (for example, McDonald's and Burger King or Hardees, IBM and Apple, Sear and K-Mart). Have students define the target market and make determination of whether the target market is the user, purchaser, or both. Have them provide a demographic description. Ask them whether there is a primary and secondary target market. What is the rationale for the chosen target market? Do the other groups in the class agree or disagree? Is there a fundamental difference in the targets?

4. List the five parameters a marketing objective must meet.

5. What is the difference between a marketing objective and an advertising objective? (Advertising objectives deal with communication issues, such as awareness and developing attitudes. Marketing objectives affect target market behavior in ways that relate directly to sales and set the tone for the whole plan.) You may have a marketing objective of increasing repeat purchase from three to five times a year, and this may be all you need to tie back to your sales objective. Latter in the plan you will need to utilize specific marketing mix tools to accomplish this marketing objective. This might be done with advertising (for which there will be objectives set) or merchandising (for which you will establish merchandise objectives).

6. Review the Dos and Don't at the end of the chapter.

CHAPTER 6

POSITIONING

Chapter Objectives

1. Define positioning, its importance, and the three major considerations when positioning the product.

2. Review the eight different types of positioning discussed in the text.

3. Review the matching, mapping, and emotional relationship methods to position a product.

4. Review how to write a succinct and meaningful positioning strategy statement.

5. Review the alternative positioning executions.

Teaching Suggestions

1. Make sure the students have read the positioning chapter before it is discussed in class. It is also important to have them develop a reference basis of what they believe positioning is and how they might go about positioning their own product. Further have the students review for their product the problems or opportunities in the marketing background section, the target market, and marketing strategies. The more immersed they are in this information, the better they can relate this chapter to their particular market situation.

2. Impress upon students that arriving at a correct positioning is critical to a product's success, because it is the "funnel" that distills all the product, target market, and strategic information into one statement. And, then it provides the overall direction for the marketing strategies and all the marketing mix tools that follow.

3. Along with having read this chapter, have each student bring to class a written list of two examples for each of the eight different "types of positioning" and have them discuss their rationale for the examples selected.

4. Take students through an example of the "How to Approach" for the matching, mapping, and emotional relationship methods. In terms of the mapping method, stress again that using primary research is always best. Have them develop their own map during a work session in class, following the three steps on pages 170 and 173 in the text.

5. Stress to students that they want to arrive at a product positioning that is not only relative to their particular market situation, but still is preemptive and meaningful, differentiating their product from the competition. This requires time and hard work. Here you have to push students to be creative because they tend to arrive at positioning statements that are general and not very distinctive.

6. Make sure students show you their application of each positioning method and stress that all students in each group participate in the positioning process.

7. Based on the outcome of the students employing the various positioning methods, have them write and share with you three different positioning statements, with each one being an emphasis variation on the product, the target market, and competition.

8. Finally, make sure that the final positioning statement is a simple statement that is concise and clearly stated. The tendency is for students to write the positioning statement as a paragraph(s). While paragraphs are very acceptable and welcome as a rationale, they are not acceptable as the positioning statement itself.

Class Discussion/Questions

1. What is positioning and why is it so critical to arrive at the correct positioning?

2. What are the three major considerations when developing a product positioning? What aspects are key to each consideration?

3. When positioning, discuss what a product's <u>real</u> attributes or benefits might be, versus how the target market <u>perceives</u> the product.

4. What is the repositioning of a product? Under what circumstances should you reposition an existing product?

5. What is a positioning gap?

6. Discuss the concept of an emotional relationship between consumers and a brand or product. Provide examples.

7. When does it make sense (if ever) to use different positioning for different target markets for the same product? (For example, Dewar's Scotch uses selective target user life-style positioning to aspiring 21 to 34 year-old men and product feature positioning to older, conservative, high income men. Each positioning was communicated in very different highly target consumer magazines.)

8. Discuss which types of positioning executions are best for certain marketing strategies. For example, positioning by problem might be best to build a market.

9. Review the Dos and Don'ts at the end of the chapter.

CHAPTER 7

MARKETING STRATEGIES

Chapter Objectives

1. Define Marketing Strategy.

2. Make sure the students understand how to develop marketing strategies.

3. Review with the students the eighteen strategic categories or considerations that must be addressed when developing a marketing plan.

Teaching Suggestions

1. There are eighteen potential strategy categories for students to consider. It is important that you stress to the students that marketing strategies describe how to meet the objectives. They also serve as an overview to the detail that follows in the marketing plan. Marketing strategies serve to direct student when the marketing mix tool sections are being developed. For example, a media marketing strategy might be to develop both a national and local media program. This media strategy provides broad direction for the marketer so that later in the media portion of the marketing plan, specifics can be developed for both national and local media plans (reach, frequency goals, media used, geography, seasonality, etc.).

   Each of the eighteen strategies should be reviewed. However, stress to the students that all eighteen might not apply to any given product. However, if a strategy category does apply, marketers should develop a broad strategy to help define the specifics which come later in the plan.

2. Discuss the importance of reviewing the problems and opportunities. Often, specific problems or opportunities can be addressed with individual strategies. It is here that students will find how important it is to have concise and meaningful problems and opportunities which summarize the many facts and figures laid out in the business review.

3. Finally, marketing R&T is an area that we stress to students. It is the lifeblood of most successful marketing organizations. However, we find that the students are very unsophisticated when it comes to developing test strategies in their plans. Here are some suggestions that will help guide their efforts.

   — Choose affordable markets, small to mid-sized DMAs.

   — Make sure you have adequate product distribution or penetration in the test market.

   — Choose markets that are self-contained from a media standpoint (minimal spill in or spill out).

— Make sure your test can translate to a national roll out (for example, that the marketing cost structure allows for an adequate sales return when rolled out to other markets).

— Utilize adequate media weight. Err on the high mark rather than using too little weight. No one wants to second guess whether it was the media weight or the test that succeeded or failed.

Class Discussion/Questions

1. Why is stealing market share easier than building the market? Make a list of firms that have successfully done one or the other.

2. Is it possible to sustain long-term growth by placing emphasis solely on a company's strengths and stronger brands?

3. Review the Dos and don'ts at the end of the chapter.

CHAPTER 8

COMMUNICATION GOALS

Chapter Objectives

1. Define Communication Goals.

2. Review the Four A's of communication and behavior, and understand the way in which each component interacts to affect one another in the target market's communication and behavior system..

3. Ensure that students understand the general concept of locking marketing objectives to individual plan tactics via awareness and attitude goals.

4. Determine how to follow the four-step process for developing individual communications goals.

5. Understand the shortcomings and challenges facing the marketer attempting to lock marketing objectives to tactical tools through the communications goals methodology.

Teaching Suggestions

1. Review the section "The Four A's of Communication Behavior" with the students (pp. 205–206). Make an overhead of Exhibit 8.1 or simply redraw it on the board. It illustrates the concept well. Be sure they understand that the basic concept of The Hierarchy of Effects is at work here -- awareness leads to attitudes which lead to behavior. But emphasize the fact that the resulting behavior *in turn* impacts additional attitudes, or reinforces the existing ones. This leads to additional behavior. This is the process that leads trial to retrial.

2. Make an overhead of Exhibit 8.2 and Exhibit 8.3. Begin with a general discussion of how sales objectives should lock quantitatively to each successive step in a marketing plan, from the marketing objectives that define the necessary *behavior* of the target market to achieve the sales goals, to the overall marketing communications goals of awareness and attitudes, to individual goals for each tactical element of the plan.

   Go through the example illustrated in Exhibit 8.3 to show how it works. This will illustrate that the sales dollars are accounted for by a certain number of purchasers -- a certain share of the target market. A slightly larger share than purchasers will express an intent to purchase; and a slightly larger share will be aware of the product and have positive attitudes, which will be comprised of pieces from each of the tactical tools.

3. Using the example in Exhibit 8.3, or using one of the students' assigned companies if it is an applications course, walk through the four step process of developing communications goals. Discuss potential sources of information for awareness results from specific tactical tools. Review the marketing objectives to determine if emphasis will be on new customers or existing ones. Review the positioning to determine the overriding attitude sought to establish attitude goals.

Based on the class discussion, apply rough numbers for overall plan communications goals for the students' business or discuss how the numbers were arrived at in Exhibit 8.3 (or both). (Understand that the students will need to provide more detail and tighten these numbers up for the final plan.) Discuss Exhibit 8.6 -- do the students agree about which tactical tools are important for generating awareness and positive attitudes? If not, make appropriate changes. Then, apply rough numbers for each of the tactical tools. Remind the students that estimates are appropriate for allocating the overall communications goals to each of the tactical tools.

At this point, you will have explained the general concept, provided a complete example, and walked the students through the process. They should be ready to attack the process on their own.

4. Discuss the last section on Communications Control Challenges. What are other potential problems one might face in the "real world" which might inhibit the students' ability to achieve individual goals? In spite of these difficulties, it is a good exercise to have students go through the entire process. Part of the learning process is facing and dealing with the shortcomings.

Class Discussion/Questions

1. What are the Four A's of communication behavior? How are they similar to The Hierarchy of Effects? How do they differ?

2. What are the marketing plan communications goals measuring? How do they lock to the sales objectives?

3. Discuss the four steps of setting communication goals. How can secondary information help?

4. In applying communications goals, what are some shortcomings one might face?

CHAPTER **9**

PRODUCT/BRANDING/ PACKAGING

Chapter Objectives

Product

1. Define the following: product, service, new product.

2. Discuss the issues affecting the product plan.

3. Determine how to establish product objectives and strategies.

4. Understand why most new products fail.

Branding

1. Define the following: brand, branding, brand equity, brand loyalty.

2. Understand the importance of branding.

3. Discuss how to establish a branding program.

Packaging

1. Define packaging.

2. Understand the different functions of packaging.

3. Review the reasons for changing a brand's package.

4. Determine how to establish packaging objectives and strategies.

Teaching Suggestions

1. The text sufficiently covers material on how to develop a product plan for an existing product. However, our students oftentimes find themselves working on a newly developed product or new product assignment. We believe that there are few businesses where new products do not represent the primary source of long-term company income and earning potential. The

development of new products is often the lifeblood of marketing-driven companies. The following will help provide a teaching framework for discussing this important topic.

a. Successful new product introductions, while always difficult in the past, have become even more difficult in the 1990s.

b. Ask students why this would be true. Reasons include:

— high cost of research and development

— shorter product life cycles which means shorter time to recapture R&D costs

— increasing cost of media to support new product introductions

— limited shelf space and distribution difficulties. With package goods, the marketer often has to buy shelf space with slotting allowances. Retailers on the other hand, have more access to product sell-through information than ten years ago and are far more sophisticated on what products receive shelf space and how much.

c. A new product program gives companies the opportunity to:

— stay competitive with product category improvement

— if current category is stagnant, enter more profitable lines or categories of business through product line expansion

— fully utilize plant capacity for manufacturers or square footage and shelf space for retailers.

— stimulate sales force and trade through introduction of something new and for them to sell and merchandise

— capture and stimulate consumers' attention through use of word "new."

— heighten or improve corporate awareness among financial community.

d. There is no one new product success formula. However, the risks are minimized and the chances for success are increased when a disciplined methodology is utilized with specific sales objectives, target market definition, and development of marketing objectives and strategies. The following steps are recommended.

Step 1: Analyze your existing business. Determine who you sell to, why your business is unique, and what your competitors are doing that is better or worse than your company. Summarize your strengths and weaknesses. Analyze how the strengths can be used in other business or product areas. Determine if the weaknesses are barriers to entry.

Step 2: Identify viable business opportunities within your business category and outside your existing business category.

Step 3: Determine the potential target market in terms of demographics, life-style characteristics, and size for each business opportunity.

Step 4: Develop a best estimate as to the unit and dollar sales potential. Develop a pro forma income statement for years one through five.

Step 5: Develop and test alternative product concepts designed to fulfill consumers needs.

Step 6: Analyze whether product features are different from existing products and whether differences are meaningful to the consumer.

Step 7: Determine the competitive environment. Analyze whether there is both direct and indirect (substitute products) competition. List competitive positioning and advertising claims. Determine competitive spending.

Step 8: Determine segmentation potential in terms of product usage; lifestyle appeal; price lines; product size, form, packaging, and channel classification.

Step 9: Determine whether distribution can be easily achieved and which channel is most appropriate.

Step 10: Determine how external influences such as government, trade restrictions, new technological inventions, and weather will affect your product.

Step 11: Estimate the affects of different price points on demand.

Step 12: Determine what existing company strengths (advertising, current distribution channels, or existing consumer franchise/customers) can be taken advantage of to hasten new product penetration of the market.

Step 13: Test the new product. Expose the concepts to focus groups. Further refine concepts in terms of name, packaging, and creative. Perform a second round of research testing prior to selected market tests.

Branding

1. There is more research on the actual new product than on its name or graphics. Names can effectively position a product, describe how a product works, or be nondefining and arbitrary, allowing the advertising to effectively create an image for the new name. However, no matter what the name's function, it is an important communication device or link to the consumers perceptions of the product. Here are some examples.

   Arbitrary: Mitchum, Ajax

   Descriptive: Soft' N Dri, Old Spice, Janitor in a Drum

   Positioning: Sure, Dial, Mr. Clean

2. Branding is an ongoing process of building and maintaining positive associations, based around the positioning for your product, its name and graphics. Discuss the elements of a brand and the branding process. Provide examples and discuss what the students associate with each.

3. Discuss the list of branding property parameters in Step 3 on page 228.

4. Have students pick an existing product category. Then have each group develop a name for a new entry into the product category by developing branding objectives, strategies, and test executions.

Packaging

1. We suggest reviewing with the students why packaging is so important—even more important today than in the past:

— Increasingly, the packaging is being called on to make a positive sales impact on the consumer in the store.

— The cost of packaging material is rising rapidly, making this an expensive component of the total product.

— Convenience is of more importance today than ever before. Often a product's convenience is realized in its packaging.

— More and more, the package is becoming an integral part of the value of the product by providing additional benefits, or by enhancing the benefits of the product.

2. Have students provide examples of packaging that was developed because of convenience (for example—Post's ziplock cereal bags; juice in 8-oz packs because of expense, disposability, shelf space stability, and less space requirement; mayonnaise in squeezable tubes (Europe); mineral water in lightweight plastic bottles; liquid soap in plastic containers).

3. Stress to students that the package is the first line in communicating the product's positioning to consumers at the point of purchase. In many categories, the majority of the purchase decision is made at the point of purchase. Therefore, packaging is critical in communicating the product's personality. Finally, effective graphics and copy can contribute towards increasing the product's perceived value and can flag promotional offers that attract the eye of the consumer.

4. The issue of legalities involved with packaging is not detailed extensively in the text, though legal protection of a brand name is touched upon in the branding section. If the package is the cornerstone of a marketing program, it needs protection from competitors. The courts are full of cases involving infringements of trademarks and copyright disputes over display panels and package designs. There are legal firms in most every major city with specialists in trademark law.

While it is said that copying is the sincerest form of flattery when it comes to packaging or branding, most companies prefer to avoid this form of flattery. Here are the steps that can be taken to offer protection:

a. Determine the type of protection that is required. Trademark registration is available for elements such as words, symbols, colors, and color combinations on the package. However, is it also possible to copyright a package for the artistic rendering and original text. Obtaining a copyright is much easier than obtaining a trademark.

b. To obtain a trademark, the marketer must undergo a lengthy process with legal fees involved. It is up to the business applying for the trademark to prove distinctiveness, for the courts will not restrict use of common descriptive words to symbols used in everyday language. The first step is to apply for a trademark (TM) — see page 234. To apply for a trademark, the goods and services must be proven to extend across state lines. In other words, the product must be used, transported, and/or purchased across state lines. The TM then becomes a registered federal trademark (circled r — ®) only after the application has been reviewed and approved.

Finally, it is important to realize that there are really two forms of protection, common law and federal registration. Common law protects companies using a name in commerce if the name has been established and used by a company over a period of time. The protection is extended for as far as the name is known. Federal protection, or trademarking, extends the rights nationwide. It is important to obtain a federal trademark if there is a chance that your name or packaging is going to be in commerce nationally. However, if you are just a local business, common law will protect your company in the area that you do business, even if at some later date a large company tries to establish a national trademark.

Note also that there are extensive federal and state regulations about what must appear on a product's package. This includes nutritional information and ingredients listings for food products, active ingredients for health products, and the use of warning statements for health or repair products or other products containing potentially hazardous materials. All of these issues, including the use of trademarks, are compounded if the product is sold in any foreign markets. Anyone developing packaging should consult a lawyer to review the materials before final production.

5. Also, remind students of the basics:

— The package should be functional for the consumer to use. It should aid in use of the product and protect the product.

— The package needs to fit on the retail shelf.

— Colors on the package should help communicate the product's positioning. If the product is a food, the packaging should have tasteful colors.

Have students develop a package design for a product and then do a little kitchen research. Go to a retailer that sells the product and ask if the package would fit on the shelf. Ask consumers what they think of the packaging and what it communicates. Talk to a broker for feedback as to the marketability of the packaging design students create.

Class Discussion/Questions

1. What are the various types of new products? When is each an appropriate growth strategy?

2. What are some common reasons for new products failing? (Underestimation of target market size; failure to adequately determine restrictions, such as government and competitive restrictions; failure to properly access consumer demand; underfunding of the marketing effort, etc.)

3. What is a brand? What is the difference between a brand and a product? Why is branding so important?

4. Strategic parameters for developing names are important so you don't get "stuck" with a name that is too restrictive. Name firms or products that in your opinion have restrictive names.

5. How do marketers make their packaging more noticeable on the shelf? What are some of the packaging innovations that provide a more convenient, disposable, easier to use, aesthetic package for the consumer?

6. Review the Dos and Dont's at the end of the chapter.

CHAPTER **10**

PRICING

Chapter Objectives

1. Define the following:

    — price

    — breakeven

    — price sensitivity

    — discriminatory pricing

    — penetration pricing

    — premium pricing

    — loss leaders

2. Discuss the considerations in pricing.

3. Determine how to establish pricing objectives and strategies.

Teaching Suggestions

1. Make sure students take time to do a competitive price analysis if the course is one of application or case study. If not, assign a product and have students do a competitive price analysis on the assigned products. Have them "shop" different stores in the market, keeping track of the price of their brand and competitive brands at each stop. One word of caution, though. Remind students to make sure that they compare apples to apples. If the product comes in different sizes, weights, shapes, or styles, make sure that the students compare only those styles, sizes, weights, or shapes that are similar when it comes to making price comparison conclusions. That's not to say it's not worthwhile to capture the complete range of pricing options and price lines, for this is actionable information. However, when students are making judgments as to price competitiveness, make sure they are making the determination based upon equal products. Also, make sure the students compare the pricing of their product relative to the competition both within stores and between stores.

2. Stress to the class that the pricing decision has an impact on four areas:

    — <u>Profitability</u>, or how much the firm will have in net profits after covering the cost of goods and the selling expenses.

— <u>Demand elasticity</u>, or how much demand (sales volume) is affected by raising and lowering the price of a product. Remember that volume can often make up for a smaller per unit margin by providing more margin dollars (For example, ten sales at $40 gross profit is better than three sales at $60 gross profit.)

— <u>Traffic generator</u>, through the use of loss leaders, or how to use pricing in conjunction with various promotion possibilities to create consumer interest and traffic.

— <u>Image/positioning</u>, or how the business can use price to help communicate the product's positioning or intended image to the target market. Further, the price helps to define the target market, and can be adjusted for the same product for different target segments.

— <u>Business goals,</u> or how different price strategies can influence short-run profits, sales growth, or even survival of a business or product.

3. Make sure your students remember the basics when setting pricing objectives and strategies.

— <u>Elasticity of demand</u>. Will the target market purchase more at a smaller price and less at a higher price? Have students talk to retailers or wholesalers and competitors in the field to get a feeling for this question.

— <u>Competitive pricing structure</u>. Make sure that students have a good perception of where their product stands in regard to price compared to the competition.

— <u>Cost of the product</u>. This important area is usually one that students have difficulty with in an applications course. For one reason, it is usually difficult to obtain good information. Included should be the cost of the merchandise if students are studying a retailer, or costs of the manufactured product if students are studying a manufacturer. For example, many retailers set costs based upon the merchandise cost as base starting point. The merchandise cost is often calculated as follows:

Gross cost of the goods or invoice cost –

discounts from the trade – quantity discounts –

season discounts – cash discounts +

transportation and stocking costs = Merchandise Cost.

The final cost of the product is determined by developing a price which will cover not only the merchandise cost but also the fixed and variable expenses associated with marketing the product in the store plus some determined amount of profit.

Obviously, this is difficult for students to obtain, especially if the product they are studying is from a private company. It may be helpful to provide students with a set range of costs (merchandise, fixed, and variable) and also with a pretax profit amount. These can usually be obtained from company financial reports from companies in the product category and serve as standards to provide students with a decision-making base. Another method is to have students develop their own ratios based upon information they find from companies in the category. This forces them to look at financial statements and wrestle with the determination of financial ratios that are the basis for pricing decisions.

Finally, remind the students that not all pricing decisions are based upon cost considerations. Some manufacturers and retailers develop a "competitive pricing" strategy of meeting the pricing of the category leaders. Still others use price to buy market share from the competition, and still others charge a premium because it helps convey a superior product, location, or service capability, or because it generates greater profit.

— <u>Product's attributes:</u> Students often forget to consider the products attributes when making pricing decisions. For example, there are many products that have inherent risks due to seasonality, perishability, or fashion orientation. A manufacturer of teenage clothing runs a real risk of the fashion going out of style. Often the strategy for both manufacturers and the retailers is to develop an initial high pricing strategy. The manufacturer may have little time to recapture design and manufacturing costs and the retailer may have to compensate for markdowns as the product loses its marketability to consumers.

— <u>Legalities:</u> Unfair trade practices are restricted by the federal government. In most cases, anything done to restrict fair trade is illegal. However, there are many examples of manufacturer price-maintenance policies. A price-maintenance policy typically involves the manufacturer suggesting the price at which the product may be marked up by the middleman and the ultimate price that the retailer may sell the price to the ultimate consumer. While such price contracts between the retailer and the manufacturer are illegal, the suggested price program is often an important part of the manufacturers distribution program. Retailers who wish to receive advertising co-op from the manufacturers or special make-up products to a retailer's specifications, find themselves in a position of being strongly encouraged to follow the suggested pricing policies.

Class Discussion/Questions

1. Why might a pricing strategy of maximizing profits be inappropriate to some marketers?

2. Provide examples of successful products or companies that have taken aggressive pricing stances, comparative pricing stances and premium pricing stances with their products. Are there other products in these same product categories that have different competitive pricing strategies?

3. Review the Dos and Don'ts at the end of the chapter.

DISTRIBUTION & PERSONAL SELLING/ SERVICE

Chapter Objectives

Distribution

1. Define distribution.

2. Discuss issues affecting the distribution decision.

3. Determine how to establish distribution objectives and strategies.

Personal Selling

1. Discuss issues affecting personal selling.

2. Determine how to establish personal selling objectives and strategies.

Teaching Suggestions

Distribution

1. It is important for students to realize there has been a revolution in the distribution or channel power between the retailer and the manufacturer. In the recent past, the manufacturer had the channel power. A strong manufacturer could practically dictate to the retailer what products the retailer displayed on its shelves. If the retailer wanted to carry the manufacturer's strong lines, it had to carry the "dogs" as well. This situation resulted primarily from the basic premise that information dictates who has control -- whoever has the data, has the power. The manufacturer had the clear picture as to the profitability and sell-through of its products. The retailer who had a multitude of products wasn't a marketer because of the difficulty of developing a selling and marketing database on a product by product basis.

Now with the advent of checkout scanners that gather and process information, the retailer has access to information on a product-by-product or unit basis. Ask a footwear retailer how many Reebok 4600s in white it sold during the third week in August and you'll get an answer. You'll also get the average turn for the shoe, the margin against budgeted margin, and more. With this type of information, competition for shelf space becomes intensified. So much so, that many manufacturers pay slotting allowances to the retailer for providing space on their shelves. And, some retailers are charging manufacturers for each sales call (especially in the grocery category).

2. In an application course, if student campaigns revolve around a package goods product, students may want to talk with local grocers concerning slotting allowances required for stocking the product. They may also want to get an idea from the grocer as to why the product receives the amount of shelf space that it does.

   If the product involves selling through a middleman, have students contact a distributor carrying the product line with a list of similar questions regarding how they approach the purchase of the product, stocking requirements, how they market the product and how they price the product for resale.

3. In an application course, if students are studying a retail store, time should be spent discussing potential distribution possibilities (advantages and disadvantages of department stores, chain stores, mass merchandisers, specialty stores, discount stores, franchise stores, supermarkets, convenience stores, off-price stores and direct mail). This information can be found in many retail marketing or management textbooks. Have each group take a category above and develop a list of advantages and disadvantages to present to the class. If the class is not an applications course, select an example product or product category and discuss the various channel options. Review the pros and cons of each, and how the packaging, merchandising, pricing, and even the product itself might be modified between channels.

4. We also suggest that you discuss market penetration with the class. Go through the penetration charts in the business review chapter on an overhead transparency so the class understands how they work. Next, stress that the numbers don't tell the whole story. Additional thoughts you may wish to convey include the following:

   — For retailers, a store's trading area includes from 75% to 85% of the store's business. This is usually obtained from an in-store survey. In addition, look at the per-capita sales ratio. For each retailer category, establish a per-capita sales number, such as $10. Once the per-capital dollar figure starts falling below the prescribed norm, start looking at whether the product is over penetrated.

   The geography and transportation network of any given market can also be studied. Often by doing this, natural trading areas become apparent. In addition, there are often social and demographic divisions within any given market that the retail marketer has to be aware of when making penetration or trading area decisions.

   After completing this information, perform the following analysis:

   a. Are there areas of the market that have a low level of competition? If so, is it because of any natural political, transportation, or demographic reasons? Are there areas where there are competitors but no reception of customers?

   b. Does the penetration analysis performed as outlined in Chapter 2 determine that the market is over- or under-penetrated?

   c. Is any given location receiving patronage from customers who are further away than the normal trading area distance for the company's stores? If so, does that store have a low sales per-capita measure?

   — For consumer goods/package goods companies, perform the following analysis:

   a. Analyze the CDI and BDI figures for the category and the company.

   b. Analyze the ACV figure (see pp. 257–258) for potential outlets in markets that have been selected for concentration based upon the CDI and BDI analysis.

   c. Develop a competitive facings (amounts of shelf space) analysis.

    d. Develop a competitive spending analysis.

    e. Make a final determination as to markets to target and outlets within the markets.

Class Discussion/Questions

1. How does the type of merchandise a retailer carries affect the size of the trading area? (Consumers will travel further for higher priced goods, those products that require special expertise of service, and those products that are special shopping goods where the customer's ego is involved in the purchase of that product.)

2. How do manufacturers use the CDI and BDI ratio to help with their distribution marketing strategies?

3. What is ACV and how is it used?

4. Discuss various problems one might face in entering new channels of distribution for a given product. Use an example, such as a consumer housware product (i.e., a blender). What problems might be faced placing the product currently in department stores to mass merchants?

5. Review the Dos and Don'ts.

Personal Selling/Service

1. If the class is an applications or case course, students should read this chapter and include personal selling objectives and strategies in their plans. We feel that it is very helpful for students to review the objectives section on page 266 and then interview companies in the field to determine realistic goals in each of the areas applicable to their products.

2. If the class is not an applications course, review the importance of the sales program and personal selling in the planning process and in the marketing mix. Personal selling represents the direct contact between the customer and the company. Further, service is becoming more and more important in differentiating brands for two primary reasons. First, technology allows competitors to more easily mimic product features, making service critical. Second, consumers are able to invest less time and effort in using products — they are generally willing to pay more to have more done *for* them. A classic example of this is the rise of the quick oil change centers from the major oil producers like Pennzoil, Valvoline and Quaker State. Discuss other examples with the class.

3. Discuss the differences in sales and service between service firms, manufacturers, or retailers. How might the service component of a consumer-oriented firm differ from a business-to-business firm? In what ways are they similar? What are the key components of sales/service objectives and strategies fofr a retail or service firms compared with those for manufacturers? Provide examples for each, and review possible objectives and strategies with the students.

Class Discussion/Questions

1. What is the overriding issue facing retailers or service firms in establishing a sales and service plan? What other issues must be addressed?

2. What are the three basic methods manufacturers use to sell their products? What are the seven factors which must be considered in determining which sales method is appropriate?

3. Discuss some of the goals which should be included in establishing selling/service objectives for a retail or service firm? For a manufacturer? What areas should be addressed in establishing strategies?

5. Review the Dos and Don'ts at the end of the chapter.

CHAPTER 13
PROMOTION/EVENTS

Chapter Objectives

1. Define the following:

   — promotion

   — consumer promotion vs. trade promotion

   — event marketing

2. Discuss the different promotion categories and the advantages and disadvantages of each.

3. Discuss the five keys to successful promotions.

4. Discuss the parameters to consider when developing promotion objectives.

5. Discuss how to develop promotion objectives.

6. Discuss the parameters to consider when developing and executing promotion strategies.

7. Discuss how to develop promotion strategies and programs.

8. Discuss event marketing, the questions asked when planning an event, and the different types of events.

9. Discuss the importance of developing alternative promotion executions and how to use the execution format as presented in the text.

10. Discuss how to determine promotional costs and how to analyze promotional paybacks.

11. Discuss how to integrate alternative promotion executions into a total promotional plan.

12. Discuss the available promotional tools and how they can be delivered to the target market.

Teaching Suggestions

1. Begin with the Appendix at the end of this chapter that defines and describes the promotional vehicles available to marketers. Next discuss the objectives, delivery methods, and advantages and disadvantages of different promotion executions. We have found that the promotion discipline is fairly foreign to students and setting the basic framework helps in further discussions on this topic.

2. Have students bring promotion examples to class, whether the example is a clipped coupon, retailer sales ad, a sweepstakes, FSI, or a bounce-back coupon. Keep these promotions pasted up

on the wall during the course of your promotion discussion and use the examples in your discussion.

3. Discuss each of the examples the students bring in. How do the examples stack up against the five keys to a successful promotion outlined on p. 273? If any of the five keys are not met, what could have been done to make the promotion better?

4. When students include promotions in outside assignments or during application of the materials, make sure they use the format in Exhibit 13.1 on page 281. This will help assure that the promotion is self-contained with specific sales and promotion objectives, strategies, a description, media and communication support, and a rationale.

5. One question that always comes up is "where do we account for the dollars that should be attributed to the promotion in the budget?" It all depends on the purpose of the promotion. If students are planning image advertising and the advertising has a coupon in it, then dollars are accounted for it in the advertising media budget. However, if the promotion is planned for incremental sales, then the promotion budget should be self-supporting. In this case the budgeted costs should include those outlined in Exhibit 13.3 on page 282 and a payback should be calculated following the example in Exhibit 13.4 on page 283.

6. Discuss event marketing. Provide examples, or ask the students to provide some. Discuss the marketer's goal. Was the event an appropriate one? Test the event against the characteristics of a successful event detailed on pages 285–286. Determine with the class whether the event could be considered a successful one.

Class Discussion/Questions

1. A closed versus open promotion was discussed. When would you use a closed promotion? An open promotion? What is the advantage of each?

2. If promotions are used for short-term incremental sales, why should marketers develop a trial-to-loyalty long-term promotion program? Provide an example of such a program. What promotion vehicles would you use at which stage of the program and why?

3. What is the danger of using a pure promotional communication strategy and not employing image-building communication?

4. What are the benefits of using events? What are the drawbacks?

5. Review the Dos and Don'ts at the end of the chapter.

CHAPTER **14**

ADVERTISING MESSAGE

Chapter Objectives

1. Define <u>advertising</u> and explain how it differs from other communication marketing mix tools.

2. Explain what is expected of advertising.

3. Review the three steps of the discipline process in developing the advertising segment of the marketing plan.

4. Detail to the students how to develop and write advertising objectives and strategies.

5. Discuss the criteria for preparing good advertising strategy.

6. Review the key advertising strategy executional elements.

7. Discuss how to select an advertising agency.

Teaching Suggestions

1. Because many students continue to confuse advertising with other communication tools, such as merchandising and publicity, clarify their meaningful differences.

2. It is worthwhile to review how advertising helps make the sale using the Three <u>A</u>s approach. First, before you can sell anything, you must make the target market <u>aware</u> of the product. Second, you must make sure the target market has the right predisposed <u>attitude</u> toward the product. Third, the target market, being aware and having a positive attitude towards a product, must be motivated to an intended behavior or <u>action</u> to buy the product. Although the Three <u>A</u>s is somewhat simplified, it provides a structure to follow and remember when the students are developing the advertising plan and executions.

3. Take students through an example of setting advertising objectives, using Exhibit 14.1 on page 301. Have students fill in the appropriate numbers as shown below.

	%	Number
Total target market	10	
Unaided/aided awareness		
Probably/definitely will purchase (attitude)		
Purchasers (trial)		

In an applications class, have the students refer back to the specific value goals set in the communications goals section. The only two real hard numbers that the student teams will have in hand (from the marketing objectives section of the plan) relate to the target market and purchaser trial. From primary research (if made available by the client), competitive spending analyses, and secondary sources, the students should work through these rough estimates to arrive at the awareness and attitude objectives which should be detailed in the communications goals. These numbers can then be used to develop specific advertising awareness goals, as detailed on page 300.

4. It is important to stress to students that time and care must be taken in developing the advertising strategy. It will be the basis for all the completed advertising materials that will be seen or heard by the target market. Remember that the advertising strategy applies to all communications, including direct mail, collateral materials, etc. (The advertising strategy is sometimes called the communications strategy for this reason.) As outlined on page 302, the strategy reflects the positioning and provides direction for a unified campaign. Within the campaign, separate "sub-strategies" may be necessary for individual tactical elements — a specific ad or point-of-sale display — or for segments of a campaign against a specific product within a brand line.

5. Review the eleven-point criteria for developing ideal strategy on pages 302–305. Go through the actual strategy examples in Example 14.2 on page 303, strongly suggesting that students follow this format if they are preparing a strategy (either as a class assignment or as part of an applications course) and that they be selective with every word they put in the strategy. For example, in the promise segment, students should list the key target market identifiers (i.e. married women 18–34) not the fully-developed target market descriptors in the target market segment of the marketing plan.

6. If the class is an applications course the students will need to develop an advertising strategy for their assigned product or business. Before writing advertising strategy, students should review the advertising objectives and even more importantly, the positioning statement as a guide to writing the strategy. Ask students to write three different promise segments of the advertising strategy in translating the positioning and then have them review with you the final strategy along with their alternates. Writing the three options forces them to broaden their perspective on how the strategy could be written and will produce a more focused final advertising strategy.

7. A good exercise, before developing advertising materials based on the strategy, is to have students complete the implementation plan in Appendix C on page 495 to enlighten them on the big picture of all advertising materials and details they will need to consider in the preparation of their complete campaign.

8. Suggest that students refer to the other advertising and ad copy/layout texts. While you may have your own preference, we have suggested two reference texts in the Campaign Course Appendix of this guide.

9. Although this is not a fundamentals course, it is a good idea to take students through the basics of developing ads and commercials.

10. Before students decide on their final campaign approach, have them review with you three different creative concepts (such as slice of life approach, testimonial, and humor) via one TV commercial and one print ad. This can be accomplished by reviewing rough "thumbnails" of student work. By having students provide the different upfront concepts, they can gain perspective on the many different ways the same creative strategy can be implemented and how their work can be enhanced. Once student teams have selected and refined a final concept, they should develop a complete package of commercials, ads, and POP materials.

11. Even if the class is not an applications course, it is useful for students to understand how the information in an implementation plan (I.P.) or creative brief translates into actual advertising materials.

Advertising should draw from the strategy and reflect the positioning and the target market, all of which should be outlined in the I.P. or brief. If the class is not an applications course, use the following exercise to help students gain direct exposure to this concept. Following is a creative brief for the development of an advertising campaign for "Medical Clinic." The next ten pages following are rough print ad concepts developed from the brief. The last page following the ad concepts is an evaluation form.

Review the brief with the students. Break the students into groups. Have them develop ad concepts based on the information provided in the brief. Then, have the groups present their best one or two concepts to the rest of the class. Hand out copies of the evaluation form, and have the other students "grade" each group using the form. They will be grading the groups' efforts in terms of how well their ad concepts reflect the positioning, target market and the strategy, as well as whether the tone was appropriate, and if the ideas were "relevant yet unexpected."

After the students have developed their ideas, presented them, and graded one another on their efforts, present the ten ad concepts provided on the following pages. These ad ideas were prepared at The Hiebing Group, using the same creative brief as the foundation. Discuss each concept with the class, specifically considering how well each ties to the strategy, positioning, etc.

12. To assist students in generating various message ideas, you might suggest they review Appendix A for idea starters (advertising message).

13. Discuss the process of selecting an ad agency with the students. Discuss why or why not a company should hire an outside ad agency.

CREATIVE BRIEF

Client: Medical Clinic

Job: Newspaper

Problem

Medical Clinic needs to build its patient base. OB and Pediatrics are key to increasing business long term.

Consumer Insight

Patients feel alienated from physicians in this era of high-technology and healthcare as big business; they long for Marcus Welby.

Positioning

Position Medical Clinic as a place that cares about patients first.

Target Audience

Women 18–34.

Key Benefit

We care about the human being. We listen. ("We" being primarily doctors, but nurses and office staff as well.)

Support for the Benefit

Care means patients are not numbers or diseases -- they are people.

Listening means hearing all the symptoms and responding to all the symptoms in some way -- medication, diet, follow-up. Acknowledging that what the patient feels or perceives is real.

OB patients have direct lines to nurses.

Pediatrics has extended office hours.

Pediatrics has a special phone line staffed by nurses.

Purpose

Medical Clinic needs to raise its visibility in the market in order to build patient counts.

Tone

Personal, uplifting

He smiled. He laughed. He cried.

Not the baby, my doctor.

This is greek text. Only for use in the layout for a visual representation of very creative copy writing. This is greek text. Only for use in the layout for a visual representation of very creative copy writing. This is greek text. This is greek text. Only for use in the layout for a visual representation of very creative copyrighting.

Medical
CLINIC

This is my miracle. I will never forget it.
Thank you, doctor, for believing in me.

This is greek text. Only for use in the layout for a visual representation of very creative copy writing.

This is greek text. Only for use in the layout for a visual representation of very creative copy writing.

This is greek text. This is greek text. Only for use in the layout for a visual representation of very creative copyrighting.

Medical
CLINIC

I'm naked,

cold, and

my legs are spread.

Please, doctor,

treat me with dignity.

This is greek text. Only for use in the layout for a visual representation of very creative copy writing. This is greek text. Only for use in the layout for a visual representation of very creative copy writing. This is greek text. This is greek text. Only for use in the layout for a visual representation of very creative copyrighting.

Medical
CLINIC

My doctor
can tell me apart

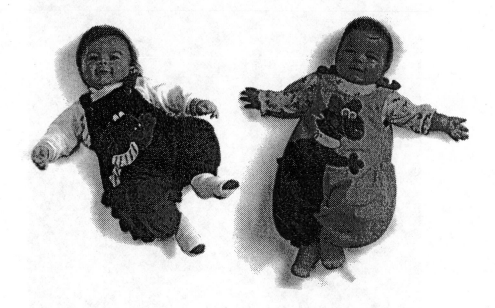

from my
twin brother.

This is greek text. Only for use in the layout for a visual representation of very creative
copywriting. This is greek text. Only for use in the layout for a visual representation of very creative
copywriting. This is greek text. This is greek text. Only for use in the layout for a visual
representation of very creative copywriting.

Medical
CLINIC

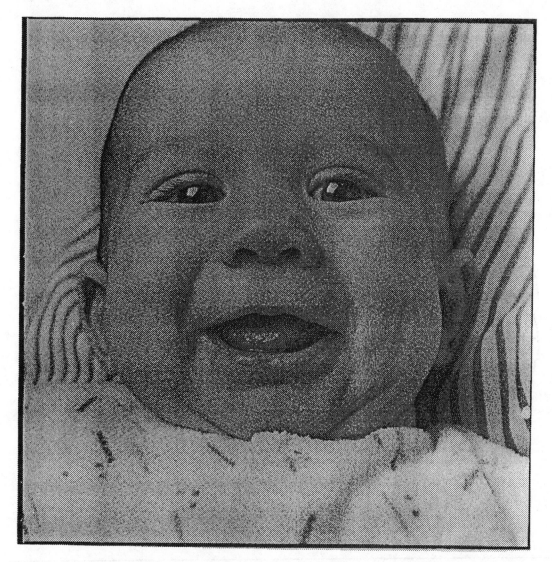

Dear Doctor, He is not a disease. He is my child.

This is greek text. Only for use in the layout for a visual representation of very creative copy writing.

This is greek text. Only for use in the layout for a visual representation of very creative copy writing.

This is greek text. This is greek text. Only for use in the layout for a visual representation of very creative copyrighting.

Medical
CLINIC

I want a doctor who knows how I feel.

This is greek text. Only for use in the layout for a visual representation of very creative copy writing.

This is greek text. Only for use in the layout for a visual representation of very creative copy writing.

This is greek text. This is greek text. Only for use in the layout for a visual representation of very creative copyrighting.

Medical
CLINIC

I want a doctor who can relate to my baby.

This is greek text. Only for use in the layout for a visual representation of very creative copy writing.

This is greek text. Only for use in the layout for a visual representation of very creative copy writing.

This is greek text. This is greek text. Only for use in the layout for a visual representation of very

creative copyrighting.

Medical
C L I N I C

Group Ad Evaluation Form

Group: _____

Score the following from 1 to 10, with 10 being the highest and 1 the lowest.

Positioning

Strategy

Tone

Relevant but unexpected

Overall presentation

Class Discussion/Questions

1. Why are advertising objectives and strategy necessary?

2. How do you measure the effectiveness of advertising? (Market research to evaluate awareness and attitude movement; copy or commercial testing for creative/communication effectiveness.)

3. What qualifies as a campaign and why are campaigns more effective than independent ads (non-related ads) for the same product?

4. When do you need different advertising strategies in addition to the campaign advertising strategy? (Trade strategy for a different target, promotion advertising strategy to communicate different benefits, such as added incentive.)

5. What is the difference between strategy and execution?

6. Review the Dos and Don'ts at the end of the chapter.

CHAPTER 15

ADVERTISING MEDIA

Chapter Objectives

1. Define the following:

    — rating points

    — reach

    — frequency

2. Generate an understanding among students for each step of the media/planning function.

3. Make sure students have an understanding of how they determine the optimum media weight levels in terms of how much is enough.

4. Students should take away the inherent value of each medium along with its respective strengths and weaknesses.

5. Make sure students can objectively evaluate one medium against the other.

6. Students should learn how to prepare the final media plan, including development of the media calendar and budget.

Teaching Suggestions

1. Define <u>media planning and buying</u>. Walk the students through the four tasks of the media planning process, beginning on page 311. This upfront preview is worthwhile because students may lose focus and become overwhelmed when they tackle this rather complex and lengthy marketing challenge. One exercise to help set the media planning structure in students' minds is to lay out the four major media planning tasks on the blackboard and have students fill in the individual steps under each of headings of background, objectives, strategies, and calendar/budget. Discuss how one step leads to another.

2. For an applications course, it's a good idea for students responsible for media coordination in each group to begin gathering the background information pertinent to the media planning function well before the planning period. This includes the information from the media audience and cost sources listed in Exhibit 15.1 on page 313. Also try to secure for your student teams, the current booklet on media costs and coverage from the media department at Leo Burnett, USA, in Chicago, IL 60601.

3. Review target market, seasonality, and geography objectives in class, specifically reviewing the factors to consider in setting geography media objectives. In terms of the CDI/BDI geographic

factors, provide example scenarios of different products asking students whether they would use an offensive or defensive strategy, or a higher or lower spending level to support their products.

4. Make sure students follow the examples and formats provided in the text when developing media objectives, media strategies, media calendar, and media budget.

5. Review terminology such as rating point, GRPs, reach, and frequency. It is also worthwhile to review, in detail, the macro and micro methodologies used to determine media weight levels and to discuss optimal reach and frequency goals for each team's product situations (Example: More or less frequency on page 320).

6. Make it clear to students that if the client provides a media budget, they should include this budget as one of the objectives. However, it is suggested that the "share of media versus share of market" and "micro target market" methods be used to gain perspective as to whether the media budget is realistic. If it is determined that the media budget given by the client is not adequate, provide the client with both a recommended and an original budget plan.

7. It's a good idea to review the Handy Media Guide (pages 326–327), particularly as it relates to relative efficiency, noticing value, reach of target audience, and pros/cons of each medium.

8. Review what should be considered for each of the major media strategies (media mix, media usage, and scheduling) and how to evaluate each medium on a quantitative basis.

9. Make sure that students understand that development of the media plan cannot take place in a vacuum but must also take into consideration the past and anticipated activities of the competition.

10. Remind students not to overlook the possibility of testing a particular medium that was not being considered for the plan because of the high risk involved or limited budget. Also, by testing a medium, such as television, the students have a reason to explore creatively another medium.

11. It will be helpful for student teams if students go through the various rough versions of alternative media plan calendars and budgets before they turn in their media plan interim report. Discuss the pros and cons of each plan. In this way, students are made aware of the many media possibilities before they decide on the final media plan.

12. The media plan, in calendar form, descriptively summarizes the plan. Accordingly make sure the students review the example of a media calendar on page 334 and the listing of media calendar inclusions on page 335.

13. Discuss the growth of direct mail, or direct response, and interactive media, as outlined in the appendix to chapter 15, beginning on page 340. What are the advantages and disadvantages of each. Stress the importance of the mailing list, and developing and maintaining a database, for the success of a direct mail program.

Class Discussion/Questions

1. What are the four given media objectives and the two optional media objectives that should be included in the media plan?

2. What is the difference between a strategic and demographic media target market descriptor?

3. What is the difference between an offensive and defensive geographic media objective?

4. What should be the media spending by market approach based on the following: (a) High BDI/High CDI; (b) High BDI/Low CDI; (c) Low BDI/High CDI; (d) Low BDI/Low CDI?

5. How do you determine reach and frequency for a particular medium without the use of the graph on page 318 for magazines, newspapers, and direct mail?

6. What is the standard reach for a 50 outdoor showing? For a 100 showing?

7. When continually adding individual mediums to the media mix (using Exhibit 15.3 on page 319), which increases at an increasing rate and which increases at a decreasing rate? (Reach increases at declining rates as it approaches 100% while frequency has no upper limit.)

8. What is the difference between macro and micro methods in determining media weight goals?

9. What is the difference between quantitative and qualitative media goals?

10. What are the difficulties of comparing the relative cost efficiency of each medium on a cost per point or cost per thousand basis? For example, the difficulty in comparing such factors as print/broadcast, size/length (1/2 page to :30), noticing values (:30 TVs superiority of attention value compared to :30 radio), and the qualitative factors on page 329.

11. What's the difference between seasonality and scheduling?

12. What questions should you ask yourself as a final check of the completed media plan? Are there any other questions to ask oneself as a final check than those on page 336?

13. What are currently drawbacks in using the internet as a medium in your media mix?

14. Review the Dos and Don'ts at the end of the chapter.

CHAPTER 16

MERCHANDISING

Chapter Objectives

1. Define merchandising.

2. Discuss the issues affecting the merchandising plan.

3. Discuss how to develop a merchandising plan.

Teaching Suggestions

1. Have students bring in examples or photographs of various merchandising techniques. Have them obtain examples of merchandising brochures from various businesses. Make sure you have examples of both personal sales presentation (brochures, sell sheets) and point-of-purchase merchandising.

2. You might want to discuss with students the different types of merchandising displays that are typically found in a retail establishment and that are used either by the retailer or the manufacturer via the retail location.

   — **Section displays:** These displays present merchandise in an environment of self-service. They are usually quite large and occupy rows of stationary aisle or wall units. This type of unit is usually very open in design to promote merchandise inspection. In general, displays are used to promote everyday merchandise. Merchandise is grouped by usage or complementary product groups. Magazine racks, grocery displays, and record displays are examples of section displays. Retailers keep detailed information on the sales per square foot of such displays and competition for shelf space with these displays from manufacturers is quite strong.

   — **Special displays:** These displays typically use premium retail space in visible, high-traffic areas of the store. They are used to draw attention to merchandise that is either being promoted by the store for a limited period to highlight the retailer's better selling goods. Examples of special displays include checkout stands, end aisles, freestanding units, and countertops.

   — **Point-of-purchase displays:** Lisa Phillips, "POP Enriched by Impulse Food Buying," Advertising Age, November 17, 1986, states that over 80% of supermarket and drugstore shoppers make their final purchasing decisions in-store and that over 60% of their purchases aren't planned. Thus, the freestanding point-of-purchase display is critical to communicate to consumers and stimulate purchase behavior in shopping environments where the consumer is making the purchase decisions without the help of a sales staff.

— **Merchandising communication:** This includes the retailer's use of bag stuffers, price signs, billboards, banners, counter signs, and copies of the newspaper ads in-store to stimulate purchase. Often the merchandising communication is further support of the broader mass communication program in newspaper, radio, or television.

— **In-store audiovisual and audio merchandising:** Many stores effectively use <u>audio communication</u> in-store to sell products and stimulate interest in consumers. K-Mart's blue light special is a good example. Shoe Carnival has a barker that continually provides shoppers with incentive to "buy now" through special three-minute promotions and special deals that focus attention on specific merchandise. Finally, Toys 'R' Us has a program called "Act Radio" — in-store broadcasts of music and advertising for products in the store. This type of merchandising not only increases the sales ratios (purchase versus nonpurchase) of these stores but also increases the amount of time a consumer stays in the store, thus increasing the chance of a purchase or multiple purchases. Audiovisual devices are also being used in stores to help entice shoppers to purchase. Audiovisual devices, such as VCRs are used to demonstrate the breadth of a product line, highlight special promotions, communicate store or product positionings, explain product attributes, communicate product pricing or demonstrate product usage.

— **Brochure display:** Brochures are often available for customers shopping for more complex products that require more information.

— **Shelf/product merchandising:** Shelf talkers, shelf banners, and product flags or displays on the product itself are commonly used by marketers to grab consumers attention at the point of purchase. Product attributes, price specials, or other promotional offers are often included in this type of merchandising.

3. Discuss the realities of implementing a merchandising program. Retailers do not want to spend a great deal of resources and time putting up and using displays, signs or other merchandising tools. Further, retailers can be particular about the size, look, and structure of materials. At the same time, retailers also generally recognize that effective merchandising support can help sell-through the product — their ultimate goal. Merchandising materials must therefore be developed within the umbrella of the brand positioning, but must also be appropriate for the retail channel or individual retailer.

4. If students are working on a project involving a manufactured product, encourage them to visit consumer outlets that will actually sell the product. Have them ask about merchandising opportunities and how the manufacturer should work with the outlet to secure merchandising space. Have them ask about the cost and any other requirements of the outlet. If students are working with a retailer, have them visit retailers in the category to study the merchandising techniques being used. Have them talk to the store manager to discern what is effective and what is not. why are some merchandising techniques used and others are not. Another worthwhile exercise is to have students talk to a company field sales representative to determine what they would like to see in terms of merchandising support. Have students incorporate this information into their final presentation.

Class Discussion/Questions

1. How is merchandising different from advertising and promotion? Why is it an often overlooked discipline?

2. What are the advantages of merchandising over advertising?

3. Review the Dos and Don'ts at the end of the chapter.

CHAPTER 17

PUBLICITY

Chapter Objectives

1. Define publicity, public relations.

2. Generate an understanding among students of the publicity tool and what it can and cannot do.

3. Students should gain an understanding of the basic issues and uses of publicity.

4. Students should understand what needs to be incorporated in publicity objectives and strategies.

Teaching Suggestions

1. Define publicity and review the "no guarantee" of this tool. Make clear that very seldom, if ever, is there such a thing as "free publicity."

2. Stress to students the need to review the problems and opportunities and the pertinent marketing strategies for their product, before developing the publicity segment of the marketing plan. Publicity should create positive awareness for a firm and its products.

3. Remind students of the importance of understanding the two targets (media and user/purchaser targets) when preparing the publicity plan.

4. A major breakdown after a publicity plan is written is the development of a "hook" that will get the attention of the media. Remind students that the hook should tie to the overall product positioning and they must push themselves to come up with ideas that will get the attention of the media and appeal to the ultimate consumer. Also, to come up with executional publicity hook ideas, you might suggest that they refer to the publicity section in Appendix A.

5. Point out to students that they will have to do more than just send out a publicity release to execute an effective publicity program. For example, they might need to develop a plan which stages an event for the purpose of gaining publicity. Or they might develop a comprehensive system of determining what trade journals need in terms of articles and then provide ongoing "expert" information and news releases as a way to assure continual publicity.

6. Many times the PSA is overlooked as an effective publicity tool. However, it should be pointed out to the students that they must tie their product to a nonprofit or charity program to generate PSA support.

7. Review the specific content of publicity objectives and strategies; then take the students through some specific examples.

8. Have each student bring two publicity examples to class and have them explain why and how they believe the product received editorial coverage.

Class Discussion/Questions

1. Why is publicity usually not as effective as advertising?

2. Discuss the different needs of various media and the need to supply different ideas and materials that best suits each particular medium.

3. What is the difference between a PSA and other forms of publicity?

4. Why are public relations and publicity not the same thing?

5. Why is it necessary to have publicity objectives and strategies?

6. Review the Dos and Don'ts at the end of the chapter.

18

MARKETING BUDGET, PAYBACK ANALYSIS, AND MARKETING CALENDAR

Chapter Objectives

1. Define payback, make sure students understand why they need a payback analysis.

2. Make sure students understand and know how to apply the three budgeting methods—task method, percent of sales, and competitive method.

3. Students should have an understanding of what goes into a marketing plan calendar and how to develop a marketing calendar that clearly communicates, visually, the many interrelated facets of the marketing plan.

Teaching Suggestions

1. Review why it is important to use two and preferably all three budgeting methods.

2. The least-used budget method will be the competitive method because it is difficult to obtain the budget data of the key competitors. However, if the text is being used for an application course, we suggest that students make some estimates of the competition's budget. Items such as production budgets, and direct mail media expenditures are often unknowns and difficult to obtain from secondary published sources. Make "best estimates" and fill these in based upon students' knowledge of the industry.

3. In order to arrive at an inclusive budget, strongly suggest that students follow the budget format in Exhibit 18.1 on pages 364 and 365.

4. Make it clear to students that it is often necessary to revise the budget based on their payback analysis, the rearrangement of the various marketing mix tools and the reconciliation with sales and profit expectations.

5. Review the different payback analyses by taking students step-by-step through the example of the retail and package good payback analysis. Emphasize that the payback analysis whether for a whole plan or one component of the plan (such as a direct mail program) may include a variety of scenarios based on different variables. As Exhibit 18.3 shows, different possible response rates to a direct mail program can change a program's contribution.

6. Review in class what is to be included in a marketing plan calendar and go through the visual example provided in Exhibit 18.5 on page 367 encouraging students to use the format provided in Appendix C.

Class Discussion/Questions

1. Why should you use more than one budget method in arriving at the final budget for the marketing plan?

2. Discuss other potential methods of analyzing the payback of marketing programs.

3. Discuss the possibility of presenting budgets with alternate plans and rationales to the client if it is determined the client-directed budget will not deliver the predetermined sales.

4. Review the Dos and Don'ts at the end of the chapter.

CHAPTER 19

PLAN EXECUTION

Chapter Objectives

1. Discuss the importance of thorough execution.

2. Make sure students understand the key steps to successful execution.

3. Ensure that students understand the importance of communicating the elements of the marketing plan throughout the organization, and for a firm to stay committed to the plan.

Teaching Suggestions

1. One aspect of marketing or marketing planning that students seem to get the least exposure to, is execution. This is unfortunate for two reasons. First, the success or failure of a plan or program hinges on its execution -- even missing the smallest detail can turn a great idea into a mediocre (or worse) program, and it is the execution that the consumers see, not the plan or ideas. Second, most students will begin their careers in very execution-oriented positions, helping to carry out the ideas and plans of their superiors. Therefore, it is critical that they understand how that role fits into the overall scheme of a firm's marketing program.

2. Review with students the three keys to successful execution of a marketing plan: adequate resources, the need for sufficient lead-time, and the requirements of all players involved to execute the program.

3. Briefly review the process of developing an activity list to illustrate the various pieces that make up a marketing plan, and the extent of individual tasks needed to implement the plan. This will give students a sense of the reality behind the plan when it comes to actually executing it. If this is an applications course, consider requiring an activity list as part of the students' final plans, to ensure that they have thought through the executional component of the plan.

4. One aspect of marketing students may not have any sense of is how it fits into the scheme of the organization. Some firms are obviously very marketing-driven, such as Proctor & Gamble or other similar consumer products firms. But while marketing may seem like it ought to be the focus of the organizations management and decision-making structure, this is not always the case. Smaller firms are particularly vulnerable to being manufacturing- rather than marketing-oriented, but there are many large, well-known firms with this characteristic. Therefore, the importance of communicating the plan throughout the organization, and gaining management support of the plan may seem self-evident, but must be stressed.

Class Discussion/Questions

1. Why is execution important?

2. What are the three keys to successful execution?

3. Review the Dos and Don'ts at the end of the chapter.

CHAPTER 20
PLAN EVALUATION

Chapter Objectives

1. Ensure that students understand, on an overall plan basis, how to evaluate the success of the plan.

2. Provide students with the methodology to evaluate their marketing plan using two alternative methods: comparative and sales trend methodology and pre- and post-research.

Teaching Suggestion

1. Review with students the basic criteria for evaluating the plan — did the plan achieve the sales and profit objectives, the marketing objectives, and the communications goals?

2. Expose the students to an evaluation methodology and discuss the importance of evaluating the results of the marketing program.

3. One method of measuring sales performance is the growth rate of improvement (GRI) process. Take students through the tasks of this process. Walk them through the examples provided in Exhibits 20.2 and 20.3.

Class Discussion

1. Review the pros and cons of each plan evaluation method.

2. Review the Dos and Don'ts at the end of the chapter.

CHAPTER 21

MARKETING RESEARCH AND TESTING (R & T)

Chapter Objectives

1. Discuss the value of testing, and when it is appropriate to test.

2. Ensure that students understand the three research and testing environments and how to best utilize each.

3. Explore the various types of testing programs, and the parameters of each.

4. Discuss the various testing techniques.

Teaching Suggestions

1. Review with students when it is appropriate to test, including the parameters to consider when determining what to test.

2. There are basically three testing environments — exploratory, experimental and in-market testing. Review these with the students. Discuss examples of each, using the examples provided on pages 393–395.

3. As the text details, you can basically test any component of your plan, from the positioning to the actual product, to individual ads or promotional programs. Discuss each of these with the students. Review methods for testing each, and how the information gathered from such a test might be used by a brand manager. For example, discuss how product use tests can assess potential purchase rates, repeat use and/or purchase, return rates, word of mouth support for the product, sources of information, and proper use and care of the product. such tests can be achieved through focus groups or one-on-one sessions, phone concept tests, or in-home use tests. Discuss these examples and the benefits or drawbacks of each, in terms of reliability, logistics, costs, and timing.

Class Discussion/Questions

Review the Dos and Don'ts at the end of the chapter.

TEST QUESTIONS AND CASES

The first part of section 2 provides you with test questions and answers. These can be used if you are using the text in a more traditional lecture class format. The questions provide broad coverage of the topics discussed in the text. They are designed to test the students' skills at *applying* the information.

The second part of section 2 is a short take-home exam. This exam involves having the students prepare a mini business review and marketing plan of their own, marketing *themselves* as a product in their efforts to obtain their first job. This has proven successful when used in marketing communications courses. It allows students to think through and apply the entire process of disciplined marketing planning, as detailed in the text, for a product they are entirely familiar with, while giving them the opportunity to think about their career goals. In a sense, this gives them a head start in that impending job hunt. Further, those students who truly "get it" tend to really enjoy this exercise. This approach is highly recommended. It can be provided in class, or as a take-home project or exam. And while the questions provided here only request a written plan, you can require your students to prepare finished resumes and other appropriate materials, based on their plans, for presentation to the class. Obviously, this section below does not include "answers" as there are no clear cut right and wrong answers. It will be your judgment in grading as to whether the students understood and properly applied the various planning steps.

The third part of this section is a detailed case, presented as a second take-home exam. The case was designed to be used in an application course format, but can be adapted and applied in a traditional lecture-oriented class. The case provides students with both primary and secondary data as well as a background section describing the company. If you choose to execute the campaigns course without obtaining actual clients, this case will serve as a starting point for students. The case combined with subsequent secondary data which students will find on the topic will provide a solid marketing decision-making base from which to build a campaign.

The case could be used as a final take-home exam or project for students in a more traditional marketing communications or marketing management lecture course. Additionally, the test questions can be used as quiz questions in a campaigns-type course.

Answer Questions 1 and 2 below using the prototype Simmons Market Research Bureau target market data, as follows:

Total Female Head of Households

Age	Total U.S. (000)	A (000)	B %	C %	D Index
Age	74,975	?B_____	100	85.7	100
18–24	?A_____	7,471	11.6	79.9	?F_____
25–34	17,130	?C_____	22.2	?E_____	97
35–44	12,512	11,066	17.2	88.4	103
45–54	11,866	10,678	16.6	90.0	105
55–64	10,905	9,698	?D_____	88.9	104
65+	13,214	11,052	17.2	83.6	98

Heavy User

	Total U.S. (000)	A (000)	B %	C %	D Index
	74,975	12,232	100	16.3	100
18–24	?A_____	973	8.0	10.4	64
25–34	17,130	2,268	18.5	13.2	81
35–44	12,512	2,919	23.9	23.3	143
45–54	11,866	2,305	18.6	19.4	119
55–64	10,905	1,978	16.2	18.1	111
65+	13,214	1,790	14.6	13.5	83

1. Fill in the blanks.

2. In the text, two segmentation criteria were discussed—volume and concentration.

    A. Define the target market in terms of volume and concentration.

    B. Provide a definition of the demographic segment you would target (provide rationale).

    C. Is the target the same from a volume and concentration standpoint in the above example?

    D. What column do you use to determine volume? What column do you use to determine concentration?

    E. What type of product category do you think this data is derived from and why?

Questions 3 and 4 are based upon the following situation:

You work for a National Certified Public Accounting Firm. The firm has hired you to develop a marketing plan. You must begin by developing a target market profile.

3. Provide a list of the questions you would need answered and provide rationale as to why you would need the information.

4. Assuming you received the information you needed, develop a methodology for determining the target market. How would you go about segmenting the target market?

Questions 5–7 are based on the data below.

Assume that there are 250,000,000 people in the United States. We're going to use this number as the population figure for the United States. Now consider the following:

National Category National Sales for Widgets: $100,000,000

DMA	Population	Sales
Chicago	8,500,000	$1,500,000
Minneapolis	2,500,000	$2,500,000
Green Bay	1,000,000	$500,000
Madison	900,000	$1,200,000

Company XX Sales of Widgets

DMA	% of Company's Population/TM	Company Sales
Chicago	61.2	$5,000,000
Minneapolis	25.2	$2,000,000
Green Bay	7.2	$1,000,000
Madison	6.5	$2,000,000

5. Define CDI and BDI. How is each used in marketing communications?

6. Calculate the CDI and BDI in the above example for each market.

7. Strategically, what would you recommend given the above situation and why?

8. Which of the following is (are) true (there may be multiple answers)? Please circle the correct answer(s).

The purpose of a situation analysis or a business is to:

A. State precisely where the firm would like to be at the end of some prescribed period of time.

B. Determine the cost of implementing a promotion strategy.

C. Develop an objective marketing database from which to use in future planning decision.

D. Identify alternative message and media strategies.

E. Identify alternative marketing communication objectives and strategies needed to positively affect the determined target market.

F. Determine and define the target market.

G. Develop an evaluation methodology to determine if the marketing communication decisions are profitable.

H. Develop a competitive analysis/information base.

9. Which of the following is (are) marketing objectives? Please circle your answer(s).

   A. Increase total unaided awareness of the brand from 15% to 30% during 1998.

   B. Increase top-of-mind awareness of the brand from 5% to 7% during 1998.

   C. Increase repeat purchases of the product from 3 times per year to 4 times, among the 18-34 male portion of the target market, during 1998.

   D. Market aggressively, with increased television weight of 200 points, during the back-to-school and Easter time periods of 1998.

   E. Achieve a sales goal of $10,500M during fiscal year 1998.

   F. Improve the attitude rating score from third in the category to second during 1998.

10. Which awareness measure most accurately predicts market share? Please circle your answer. Then briefly explain why.

    A. Unaided awareness.

    B. First mention unaided awareness.

    C. Total awareness.

    D. Predictor awareness.

11. There was great emphasis put on developing positioning both in the text and in class. We discussed three ways to actually develop positioning: matching, mapping, and emotional relationship. Describe how any one of these techniques works. Provide an example of a product and make up a list of competitors and the information you need to complete an example.

    From your example, analyze the situation and explain what the positioning of your example company should be and why.

    Now list six executional ways to develop a positioning. Select one of these and develop a positioning concept. You will be graded based upon whether the positioning ties back to your example above, and in the completeness and persuasiveness of your answer.

12. In the example below, a facial tissue company has come to you and has asked that you create additional uses for their Specialty packs—Travelers (targeting car users/travelers), Pockets (targeting women with purses), Keen Teens (targeting teens and use in teen bedrooms), and Macho Size Tissues (oversized tissues for macho men).

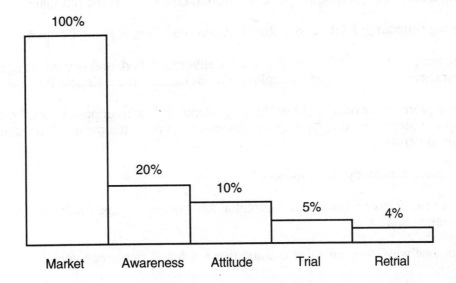

100%

20%

10%

5%

4%

Market   Awareness   Attitude   Trial   Retrial

Provide the top two questions you would ask before making a recommendation. Then make up answers for the questions.

Now with the answers to your questions and the above chart, give a solution to the problem. Would you recommend development of alternative uses for the products (for example, travelers used by children going to school) or would you stay with the same usage pattern?

Depending upon your answer above, write a marketing communication idea for achieving your goal. You will be graded on the strategic ramification of your idea as well as the idea itself. If your solution is to use promotion, provide a tactical example as well. For example, a promotion utilizing initial sampling to all teenage girls via direct mail delivery.

13. Trace the effect on the target market and advertising strategies from the movement of a product through the product life cycle. Relate the answer to a product going through introduction, growth, and maturity.

Answer Questions 14–16 using the information below:

You are a retailer and the average shoe sells at $35. Fixed costs are $15,000 per month, variable costs are $20 per shoe.

14. How many shoes must be sold at $35 to lower costs each month?

15. Now assume the retailer is selling above breakeven at 2,000 pairs per month. What are the profits per month?

16. Now assume that through past experience you estimate that a drop in price per shoe to $30 will result in a 30% increase in business. Will profits increase? Prove it.

17. What is ACV? How do package goods firms use this term to help define their distribution objectives and strategies?

18. What is an open promotion? What is a closed promotion? When would each be used?

19. Develop a set of data that proves you know how to calculate the cost of a coupon. (Use a 50¢ coupon and develop a format for determining the cost of redemption for that coupon.)

20. Develop a complete promotion execution from theme through the rationale.

21. Define the following: ROP; Cross-Ruff Coupon; FSI; Bonus Pack; Coupon.

    Provide the promotion objective, execution delivery method, and two advantages and disadvantages for: Couponing; Sampling; Premiums; Refunds; Repeat Purchase Offers.

22. Choose a product. Develop a list of three problems and three opportunities. From this list, develop a strategic creative strategy or promise, a support statement, a tone statement and rationale statement.

23. Define reach, frequency, and GRPs.

24. Why does radio have a lower reach potential and higher average frequency than other mediums, such as television?

25. Describe one way of establishing quantitative reach and frequency goals.

26. You are a marketer who is trying to determine the amount of frequency needed to successfully market your product. Name five factors that will determine if you use more or less frequency (name five that would lead you to use more and five that would lead you to use less).

27. Define the term <u>noticing values</u>. List the following mediums in order of their noticing value (from most to least): Radio; Television; Local newspaper; Direct mail.

28. Describe at least three of the key steps to successful execution of a marketing plan. Explain how you might go about implementing these steps and why each is important.

29. Provide a description of the Growth Rate of Improvement Evaluation methodology. How are the three stages, preperiod, test period, and postperiod used in this methodology?

30. Use the following data from an actual test situation and develop a GRI analysis. What do you recommend based upon the data?

Analysis of Charlotte Promotion

CHARLOTTE PROMOTION	CHARLOTTE MEDIA SUPPORT	CHARLOTTE MEDIA COST	WEEK END	1988-CHARLOTTE $ FOR $ SALES	1987-CHARLOTTE $ FOR $ SALES	% CHANGE CHARLOTTE	1988-SYSTEM $ FOR $ SALES	1987-SYSTEM $ FOR $ SALES	% CHANGE SYSTEM
			1/2/88	$44,052	$40,354	9.18	$2,046,086	$3,096,036	-8.07
			1/9/88	$18,696	$29,333	-36.26	$1,945,163	$2,514,659	-22.65
			1/16/88	$27,898	$30,944	-9.84	$2,160,774	$2,465,987	-12.38
			1/23/88	$32,614	$25,480	28.00	$2,253,873	$2,154,112	44.63
			1/30/88	$29,079	$26,764	8.65	$2,097,441	$2,103,515	-0.29
			2/6/88	$31,763	$30,280	4.89	$2,201,272	$2,267,011	-2.90
14 WEEKS TRENDING IN			2/13/88	$25,365	$32,113	-21.01	$2,035,578	$2,383,300	-14.59
			2/20/88	$29,428	$26,937	9.25	$2,246,779	$2,416,292	-7.02
			2/27/88	$28,452	$31,448	-9.53	$2,278,464	$2,583,404	-7.02
			3/5/88	$32,747	$37,290	-12.18	$2,572,484	$2,878,403	-10.63
	TV: 150 PTS*	$4,765	3/12/88	$40,244	$39,751	1.24	$2,915,777	$2,808,410	3.82
	TV: 150 PTS*	$4,765	3/19/88	$39,745	$43,306	-8.22	$2,868,512	$3,086,136	-7.05
			3/26/88	$42,910	$41,142	4.30	$3,078,141	$3,210,042	-4.11
			4/2/88	$68,522	$48,593	41.01	$4,640,118	$2,981,636	55.62
CHARLOTTE IMAGE	TV: 150 PTS	$5,620	4/9/88	$40,926	$47,703	-14.21	$3,039,304	$3,281,500	-7.38
	TV: 150 PTS	$5,620	4/16/88	$40,743	$80,956	-49.67	$3,041,311	$3,281,500	-7.32
			4/23/88	$40,034	$40,717	-1.68	$3,135,590	$2,825,544	10.97
			4/30/88	$38,518	$40,747	-5.47	$2,724,411	$3,060,500	-10.98
CONCEPT	TV: 100 PTS	$3,945	5/7/88	$36,158	$46,507	-22.25	$2,887,624	$3,055,161	-5.48
	TV: 100 PTS	$4,570	5/14/88	$37,555	$44,999	-16.54	$2,717,203	$3,132,419	-13.26
	TV: 100 PTS	$4,230	5/21/88	$40,460	$43,317	-6.60	$2,900,329	$3,098,067	-6.38
			5/28/88	$38,711	$44,598	-13.20	$2,810,430	$2,940,321	-4.42
	TV: 100 PTS	$2,910	6/4/88	$37,912	$45,649	-16.95	$2,802,664	$3,014,247	-7.02
	TV: 100 PTS	$4,035	6/11/88	$40,341	$42,897	-5.96	$3,042,419	$2,913,323	4.43

* Mainline Advertising

TOTALS	1988-CHARLOTTE $ FOR $ SALES	1987-CHARLOTTE $ FOR $ SALES	% CHANGE CHARLOTTE	1988-SYSTEM $ FOR $ SALES	1987-SYSTEM $ FOR $ SALES	% CHANGE SYSTEM
PRE-PERIOD	$491,515	$483,735	1.61	$36,140,462	$36,948,943	-2.19
PROMOTION	$391,358	$478,090	-18.14	$29,101,285	$30,602,582	-4.91

MEDIA/SALES RATIO	CHARLOTTE MEDIA COSTS	CHARLOTTE SALES	CHARLOTTE MEDIA/SALES RATIO	SYSTEM MEDIA COSTS	SYSTEM SALES	SYSTEM MEDIA/SALES RATIO
Pre-Period	$9,530	$491,515	1.94%	$1,060,500	$36,140,462	2.93%
Promotion	$30,930	$391,358	7.90%	$1,227,900	$29,101,285	4.22%

129

The purpose of the Charlotte analysis is to determine whether the :30 concept spot produces stronger sales and greater profits than the mainline promotion schedule. The :30 concept test comprised of running 800 TRPs of solely :30 concept television spots from April 9, 1988, to June 11, 1988, at a cost of $30,930. This analysis should review sales results for the Charlotte DMA prior to and during the Charlotte :30 concept test. It should also compare these results to all retail stores in the system.

Methodology and tables for analysis

In preparing the image concept analysis, three months of trending in data acts as a pretest period. However, since the promotional period ended only recently, no data is available to act as a post test.

All sales figures are store-for-store sales taken from the DMA reports. The Charlotte television media costs are actual costs incurred taken from the Current Announcement Schedules. Total system sales and costs consist of all media which ran in all markets, including special promotions, such as grand openings and the :30 concept test in Charlotte.

Answers

1. A. 8,348 (add up demographic columns 25-34 through 65+ and subtract from 74,975)

   B. 64,266 (85.7% times 74,975)

   C. 14,301 (add up demographic columns below 64,266, subtract from 64,266)

   D. 15.09 (9,698 divided by 64,266)

   E. 83.49 (14,301 divided by 17,130)

   F. 93.23 (79.9 divided by 85.7)

2. A. The segments accounting for the greatest volume and most quickly totaling 50% of the volume (the goal in establishing a target market) would be the age groups of 25–54. This is true for the heavy user as well as the all user categories. The greatest concentration of users would be in the 35–64 age groups.

   B. Look for students to acknowledge the heavy-user segment data. The most likely target would be heavy users ages 35–64. Acknowledge that these users are probably families because of the concentration skews towards the middle age—thus most likely showing the existence of children and a family unit.

   C. The target from a purely volume standpoint would be heavy users 25–54. When concentration is also considered, it would be wise to add the 55–64 age group and either keep or subtract out the 25–34 age group.

   D. B for volume, C and D for concentration.

   E. A household product category that receives use by all demographics, but receives heavier use from female head of households with families.

3. See text pages 89–92.

4. See text pages 89–926.

5. See pages 100–101 in the text.

6. **National Category Sales for Widgets: $100,000,000**

DMA	Population		Sales		CDI
Chicago	8,500,000	3.40%	$1,500,000	1.5%	44 (1.5/3.4)
Minneapolis	2,500,000	1.00%	$2,500,000	1.5%	250
Green Bay	1,000,000	0.40%	$ 500,000	0.5%	125
Madison	900,000	0.36%	$1,200,000	1.2%	333

Company XXX Sales of Widgets

DMA	% of Company's Population/TM	Company Sales		BDI
Chicago	61.2	$5,000,000	50%	81.7
Minneapolis	25.2	$2,000,000	20%	79.4
Green Bay	7.2	$1,000,000	10%	139.0
Madison	6.5	$2,000,000	20%	308.0

7. Investment spend in Minneapolis due to high CDI and low BDI. This would include an increased emphasis in terms of distribution and advertising/promotion/media budgeting. Continue to support Madison with existing higher levels of spending. Potentially pull back some in Green Bay (100 CDI with a 139 BDI) and do not support Chicago as much as in the past or in other markets.

8. C and H only. See disciplined campaign development chart on page xiii and discussion of the business review on page 4.

9. C only. See marketing objectives discussion, pages 151–153. Remind students that marketing objectives must affect consumer behavior and directly tie to sales (review Exhibit 5.9 on page 156).

10. B

11. See page 162 and following in the text.

12. There should be a convincing discussion regarding the fact that there is little awareness for the product, yet a strong trial/retrial ratio. From this fact, the marketing objective of establishing new trial against the existing target market profile (nonusers on the product) would be appropriate. The strategy should not be one of expanding product uses but in building trial of the product for the existing uses. The rationale would be that there is a small amount of awareness, a small amount of trial but a strong trial/retrial ratio. Therefore before trying to get consumers to use the product for different uses, place efforts in building trial against current uses for the product, uses that seem to be very satisfactory.

13. See text pages 97–98.

14. P = price, VC = variable cost, FC = fixed cost, X = volume of units at breakeven.

    $35X = $15,000 + $20X

    $15X = $15,000

    X = 1,000 pairs.

15. 2,000 = number of shoes sold

2,000 x $35 = $70,000
$15,000 = $20 (2000) = cost = $55,000
Profit = $70,000 – $55,000 = $15,000.

16. 1.3 x 2,000 = 2,600 number of shoes
2,600 x 30 = $78,000
$15,000 + $20 (2600) = $67,000 costs
$78,000 – $67,000 = $11,000.
Profit went down $4000 from the $15,000 previously stated.

17. See chapter on distribution, beginning on text page 256.

18–21. See Promotion chapter, pages 278, 282, and 290–297.

22. See text page 301–303.

23. See text pages 316–317.

24. Radio is a relatively fragmented medium with individual stations attracting narrower target audiences. It does not provide the broad reach against a mass audience that television does. Therefore, the same number of messages on radio versus television would reach fewer people more frequently.

25. See text pages 318–324.

26. See chart on text page 320.

27. See text pages 326–328.

28. See text pages 375–379.

29. See text pages 387–388.

30.

GRI	PRE %	TEST %	GAIN/LOSS % POINT
CHARLOTTE	1.61	–18.14	–19.75
SYSTEM	–2.19	–4.91	–2.72
		GRI	–17.03

You are a product. If you don't believe it, wait until you interview for that first job. If marketed properly, you'll do very well securing a job in a field that excites you and where you'll be well-compensated over time. You'll also find plenty of growth opportunities. To accomplish this, you need to apply the disciplined marketing planning methodology, preparing a business review of information, and developing a plan of attack for marketing yourself to prospective employers.

This is your assignment. Considering yourself as a product, prospective employers as "consumers," and other job-hunters as your competition, develop a business review and marketing plan, as detailed below. Include explanations and rationale whenever possible. Where you would normally supply hard data, explain what data you would seek to obtain and why. Make assumptions when necessary and simply state what those assumptions are. For example, attitude and attribute preferences can be estimated for this exercise, and plan elements developed based on your estimates.

1. Develop a scope for your business (your job hunt).

   — List key strengths and weaknesses.

   — Develop core competencies.

   — Develop alternative industry target markets.

   — Provide an analysis and rationale as to why you are choosing your selected scope and industry target market.

2. The next two steps of the business review include Product and Market Review and Target Market Effectors. Creatively explain what information you would use, how you would develop it, and how it will help you later in your plan. Try to utilize as many of the tasks outlined in the text as possible. Present this in a simple outline form, rather than lengthy prose.

3. Create a list of relevant problems and opportunities, based on your proposed business review outline.

4. Outline your target market and marketing objectives.

   — What businesses are you going to target and why? (Your rationale here should be based on the information provided in your business review.) Who are the decision makers, and who are the influencers you will need to reach?

   — Be creative in developing marketing objectives. Remember the definition of a marketing objectives and apply this to the job market. State your goals simply and clearly, but provide rationale and explanation as appropriate to support your decisions.

5. Develop a positioning of yourself for the job market.

   — Use the mapping, matching or emotional relationship approaches -- show the steps you would take, and make assumptions of what the situation really is in your case.

   — Begin with your positioning statement -- make sure it is clear and concise. Then, follow with the rationale for your positioning using the approach you've taken to support your position.

6. Develop marketing strategies which help you communicate your positioning and achieve your marketing objectives. Present at least five strategies, not including advertising strategies (see 7, below). Examples might include competitive strategies, target market strategies, or personal selling strategies.

7. Develop an advertising message plan.

 — Include awareness and attitude objectives.

 — Develop an advertising strategy, as laid out in the text. This should include a promise, support, tone and rationale.

 — Include executional considerations, if appropriate.

This project is meant to make you think, allow you the flexibility of answering the questions from the standpoint of your career goals in marketing communication, and at the same time allow you to more fully explore topics we have discussed in lecture and you have read in the text assignments. Be strategic first and then be creative. Most importantly, utilize the methodology presented in the text to develop a strategic, idea-oriented marketing communication plan.

Background

The following data is fictitious. There is no correlation to real life information.

You are the Marketing Director for a retailer called Seth Cooper of Heartland. Seth's is an off-price menswear store which carries brand name suits and sport coats for less. The stores look very institutional with racks of suits and menswear and brand name signage on the walls above the racks. Each store is approximately 5000 square feet. The stores are located in strip centers. The stores are serviced by salespeople and there is a tailor shop in the rear of each store. Although the store carries suits and sports coats in all price ranges, it emphasizes the lower-end merchandise in its merchandising, pricing, and advertising/promotion. The chain has four stores in Detroit, one in Ann Arbor, and two stores in Indianapolis. The stores are averaging $550,000 per store with flat sales the past three years. They need to gross approximately $630,000 to break even. The average margin is 46%. In addition, the following data is available to you.

Results of Primary Marketwide Telephone Research in Detroit

1. The incidence of suit or sport coat purchase in the past two years in 32%

2. Male purchasers of suits and sport coats were categorized into <u>shopper types</u>. Department stores including chain stores (34%), men's specialty stores excluding discount or off-price stores (28%), and shoppers who shop at a variety of store types (33%). The remaining 5% of the sample were classified as off-price store shoppers.

3. The major department store, Hudson's (61%), and national chains, Sears (38%) and Penney's (32%), dominated <u>total awareness</u>. Many specialty stores were mentioned, none of which stood above the rest or approached Hudson's, Penney's, or Sears. Among the specialty stores, Kosin's (12%) and Osmum's (9%) appeared to be the major competitors. Yet even among the breakout of men's specialty store shoppers, Hudson's had higher total awareness levels than did Kosin's and Osmum's (38% vs. 234% and 18%).

   In addition, Hudson's and the more prominent men's specialty stores tended to have higher awareness among heavy purchasers while the national chains had higher awareness among the light purchasers. Awareness of off-price menswear stores selling suites and sport coasts was very low. <u>First mention awareness</u> scores, though lower, had the same relative ranking as the total awareness figures.

4. Quality was considered to be the most <u>important attribute</u> when choosing a store at which to buy men's suits and sport coats. Heavy users placed even more emphasis on quality. Value and selection of styles and sizes were next most important. Customer service and low prices were ranked fourth and fifth. Selection of nationally advertised brands and convenient location were relatively least important.

5. Only half of the male sample purchase a suit or sport coat once or more a year. Only 32% of males contacted qualified for inclusion in the study based upon a purchase of a suit coat or sport coat in the past two years. Specialty store shoppers had the highest <u>frequency of purchase</u>.

6. The purchase of a suit or sport coat is a planned event. Eight-five percent of the suits or sport coats last purchased by respondents were planned and only 15% were impulse.

7. Women have a major influence on the purchase of a suit or sport coat. Only 38% of the male respondents claimed they were the only ones involved in the suit or sport coat purchase. Spouses of heavy purchasers had less influence on the purchase of a suit or sport coat although 47% were involved in the decision making process.

8. Respondents normally shopped at one to two stores for a men's suit or sport coat. Heavy purchasers and combination shoppers shopped at a greater variety of stores than the average shopper. Female shoppers were more likely to shop at department stores. Light purchasers were more likely to shop at the national chains.

9. Hudson's and Sears were the only two stores to have last purchase shares greater than 10%.

10. Total yearly visits to menswear stores were about 22. The individuals who bought sport or suit coats during one of these visits bought 1.5 times per year.

11. Even among the specialty stores only breakout (when looking at those men who consider specialty stores the main place they shop for menswear), department stores and a high level of visits compared to specialty stores (the broad merchandise mix in department stores results in multiple visits). The specialty stores shares increased when considering suit or sport coat purchases as opposed to share of visits.

12. On average, male respondents made a menswear purchase on 46% of their visits. Women had a purchase ratio of 66%. Of total menswear purchases, 30% resulted in a suit or sport coat purchase, 42% for heavy users. The specialty stores rated much higher in purchase ratios.

13. The suit or sport coat purchaser can be described as follows: Married, median age of 40-44, median household income of $35,000 with a white collar occupation.

In-Store Research

1. The in-store survey showed that total traffic at Seth's was low. And while the store features sport and suit coats, less than half the unit purchases were these items. Ties and pants were purchased by the largest percentage of the sample.

2. Price was the most important reason for purchasing at Seth's.

3. The mean number of visits to Seth's in the past six months was 2.1 and the mean number of purchases was 0.8. Of the total market visits made by Seth's customers 20% were made to Seth's. Department stores were receiving the greatest number of visits by Seth's customers.

Secondary Data/Business Review Information

(Note: this is a summary of secondary and primary research information. There are times when the secondary numbers do not correspond to the primary research findings in the absolute, though directionally there are no differences. In addition, when primary research is summarized, it is stated as such. All other statements apply to secondary information.)

1. Men's suit and sport coat market constitutes a relatively limited market. Total purchases of suits and sport coats by males in a given year are low in the absolute and the category has low purchase rates when compared to most other nondurable consumer goods. In addition, while

small percentages of males purchase any suits or sport coats in a given year, the majority of those purchasers only purchase one suit or sport coat per year.

— Limited incidence of purchases/limited total purchases. (30MM suits and sport coats purchased per year/approximately .4 suit and sport coat purchased per male 18 plus per year.)

— Limited number of purchasers. (Only approximately 25% of the men purchase a suit or sport coat in any given 12-month period. There is a long purchase cycle for suits and sport coats. A small percentage of consumers purchase more that one suit or sport coat in a given year.)

2. The low purchase rates suggest that potential purchasers of suits and sport coats have an especially low <u>share of mind</u> (awareness) with the products except during relatively infrequent purchase periods.

3. <u>Awareness</u> for men's apparel stores, with very few exceptions, are low. There exist many outlet alternatives for consumers with a high degree of communication clutter; ;very few outlets are making an impact. (It appears that Seth's has very low to nonexistent unaided awareness levels.) This is particularly the case in newer markets.

4. The potential <u>target market</u> for suits and sport coats is broad. Establishing a well defined target market for Seth's will be difficult and expensive.

— The potential target market for suit and sport coat purchasers is broad, encompassing a large segment of the male population 25–54. Yet suit purchasers are not homogeneous; they purchase suits and sport coats at different frequencies, for different needs, and at different price ranges.

— The 35–54 year-old age group which has the greatest propensity to purchase a suit or sport coat (has the largest <u>concentration</u> of purchasers), is not the same as the 25–34 age group which has the largest number of purchasers (has the largest <u>volume</u> of suit purchasers).

— Heavy purchasers of suits and sport coats represent a smaller percentage of total purchases (22% purchase 46% of the units) than most consumer categories.

— Heavy users/purchasers of suits and sport coats and normal purchasers have similar attribute wants and demographics. However, heavy users have even more upscale demographics than do normal users and they rate quality as even more important relative to other product attributes than do normal users.

— Target market identification is even further complicated because of the female influence in the purchase decision. Women are an important influence in the purchase of men's clothing in general and a significant influence in the specific purchase of men's suits and sport coats. Research demonstrates that women are also important influences in store selection decisions.

5. The <u>total men's and boys' apparel category</u> is not a growth category. It has maintained static to declining trends in units sold over the past five years.

6. Men's and boys' suits have declined during the same period at even greater rates than the total <u>apparel category</u>.

7. Seth's product and sales <u>mix</u> demonstrates a heavy dominance of suits, sport coats, and dresswear. Yet nationally, casual wear, sportswear and athletic wear constitute the majority of clothing purchased. And unlike the apparel category in the aggregate, these categories increased in units sold and per capita units sold over the past five years. In summary, Seth's does not sell a full line of clothing which appeals to the largest market or is experiencing the greatest growth.

8. By placing emphasis more on suits and sport coats and essentially ignoring all other clothing options, Seth's is obtaining larger ticket sales but is severely limiting its <u>trial and repeat</u> potential.

9. Seth's primarily focuses on suits versus even sport coats. Nationally more sport coats than suits are sold among apparel outlets, though suits account for greater total sales volume. The national average is 1.7 sport coats for every suit sold. Comparatively, Seth's is selling fewer sport coats than suits (.79 sport coat for every suit sold).

10. Primary research shows that Seth's stores have low traffic overall and lower <u>purchase ratios</u> compared to the competition. In addition the Seth's customer is not loyal, shopping other chain and department stores first for menswear.

11. The majority of Seth's suits and sport coats fall in the mid-to-lower <u>price range</u>. This price range has shown a decline in units relative to other price categories in the suit market. The higher price suits, which Seth's does not carry as much of and does not emphasize, have experienced growth within the suit category during the past five years.

12. The <u>heavy suit purchaser</u> most likely does not fit the Seth's concept.

   — Has even more upscale demographics than normal suit purchasers.

   — Shops traditional specialty stores.

   — Rates quality as even more of a purchase factor than the normal suit purchaser does.

   — Shops more often for menswear. Seth's has a light visit concept because of its merchandise and pricing mix.

   — Price is even less of a factor than with normal purchasers. Again, with normal purchasers, price was not the major factor.

13. Primary research demonstrates that Seth's receives average <u>selection ratings</u> and low quality ratings in the market wide survey. Both are extremely important to the suit and sport coat purchaser.

14. There exist strong <u>seasonal patterns</u> of distribution and retail consumer sales. Seth's seasonality of sales is even more severe than the seasonality of men's apparel stores nationally. Seth's primary selling season is the October through holiday season.

15. Nationally, while popular outlets for men's and boys' clothing and outerwear sales in general, <u>discount stores</u> do not receive the greatest percentage of suit and sport coat sales. Nationally the discount store market share for suit sales is 10% for units and 7% for dollars. Men's specialty stores account for the greatest percentage of men's suit purchases with a market share of 36% unit and 48% volume. The same relationship holds true for sport coats with the exception that both department stores and specialty stores dominate sport coat purchases.

16. Outlets such as Kuppenheimers are <u>fragmenting</u> an already small market for <u>off-price suits and sport coats</u>. And to a certain extent they have preempted the market.

17. Seth's has <u>no reason for being other than price</u>. And department stores and national chains are starting to act more and more like off-price outlets with frequent discounting and sales.

18. It appears people buy the store <u>before the label</u>.

19. The purchase of suits and sport coats is a <u>planned event</u>.

20. While Seth's customers are not <u>loyal</u>, shoppers of men's apparel stores appear to be relatively loyal.

21. There exists a lower than expected <u>customer transaction</u> purchase amount at Seth's given the merchandise mix favoring suits. (Average customer transaction: approximately $100.)

22. The overall look of the <u>advertising</u> is not one of quality and is cluttered with phrases such as "doorbuster specials" and "now you have buying power." In addition, there does not seem to be a consistent focus on a basic selling idea/theme line with phrases such as "44 brand names for less," "we make expensive clothing affordable," and "wool, it's affordable."

Exercises

1. What other information do you need to complete the business review? List your questions and provide answers based upon additional research you re able to uncover. (Or, if you re unable to uncover the information, provide what you think to be logical answers. Then use this information in building the rest of your plan.) Follow the questions at the end of each business review step as a guide.

2. Develop a list of problems and opportunities from which you will develop your marketing plan.

3. Develop sales objectives for the company.

4. Develop a target market, marketing objectives, marketing strategies and a positioning strategy for the company. Include a brief rationale for each objective and strategy. Utilize a matching or mapping exhibit as part of your rationale for the positioning strategy.

5. Develop the rest of the plan utilizing the marketing mix tools you feel appropriate. For each marketing mix tool you use, provide objectives, strategies, and a rationale.

6. Provide a marketing budget, calendar, and payback analysis for your plan.

7. Provide an evaluation methodology.

THE CAMPAIGNS COURSE

INTRODUCTION

The objective of the campaigns course is to give students the opportunity to apply their skills and learning from previous marketing and communication courses through the development of a marketing-based advertising and promotional campaign. This will be accomplished by working as an account team in a real-world environment fostered by the instructor and the course structure. The course is composed of four parts.

1. **Marketing Background**—Gathering of relevant data in the form of a business review or situational analysis and summarizing this data into a list of problems and opportunities.

2. **Marketing Plan**—Preparing each plan segment with objectives, strategies, and rationale. The plan is constructed in a building block fashion into an integrated and comprehensive marketing plan—the foundation for the execution of a campaign.

3. **Campaign Preparation**—Preparing and executing a stand-up summary presentation, and preparing a final, written marketing program, including campaign execution.

The example syllabus following this introduction provides an overview of the course. This should be read before further. It can easily be adapted to fit your own individual style of instruction while keeping the basic structure of the course intact.

You might also want to keep in mind as you read through this manual and corresponding text that the authors have taken a very pointed stand and share their views on what is important both in the teaching of this course and in the preparing of a successful marketing plan and campaign. Accordingly, the authors acknowledge that there are many different means to accomplish a successful campaign and welcome any and all suggestions that may improve the manual and the text.

In order to make this course authentic to a real-world marketing situation and campaign development, you should:

1. Encourage communication/journalism, business, and art students to enroll in the course. This course provides the most optimum learning opportunity in a multidiscipline classroom environment.

2. Divide your class into account teams comprised of students from each discipline, with approximately five to seven students per team.

3. Whenever possible, create a competitive environment between teams. For example, 36 students could be divided into six agency teams with three teams competing against each other on the same product, and the other three teams competing against each other on different products. Although we are proponents of instilling competitive reality to the course, we have also seen students develop quality campaigns with *each* team developing a marketing program and campaign for a *different* product.

4. Make sure students understand the many assignment deadlines and meet them without exception. This is necessary to make a compete, quality campaign a reality, while giving students a taste of the fast moving marketing and advertising world and exposing them to similar deadlines faced in the real world.

Example Syllabus

PROMOTIONAL CAMPAIGNS

Course #:
Location:
Day/Time:
Instructor:
Semester:
Office:
Office Hours:
Office Phone:

Prerequisites for Promotional Campaigns: Introductory marketing or advertising course. Lots of time. Desire to work as a team on an unstructured marketing project.

Promotional Campaigns is a project course which allows students to apply the theory and techniques developed in several journalism, business, and art courses. There is one assignment in the course: the develop a campaign based on a marketing plan for a firm while working in an account team made up of students with varying backgrounds.

You will be assigned to a product team and work as an advertising agency in preparing a marketing plan, along with a comprehensive communications campaign, and preparing and producing the marketing communication materials for the product assigned to your agency.

Each member of the agency will assume specific duties and the responsibilities for specific areas of the campaign. These areas include marketing; market research; creative; media; sales promotion; merchandising; and public relations. In so doing, you will become acquainted with the activities and functions of advertising agencies. You will also experience the strategic details and pressures of deadlines that are inherent in the planning, preparation, and execution of an actual promotional effort.

Each agency will rehearse its campaign presentation in class the week prior to the final presentation. Each agency will give its presentation during the final week of class to a Plans Board, comprised of the client and other professional advertising and marketing people.

Classroom Approach

Four classroom formats will be employed.

1. Several speakers from the marketing and advertising industries will present information and materials on various aspects of the advertising business. The speakers and topics will be announced in class. These presentations will be during regularly scheduled class.

2. Lectures by the instructor.

3. Review sessions between each team and the instructor.

4. Individual team work sessions.

Grade Determination

There will be no exams in this course. However, there might be an occasional quiz. Ninety-five percent of the grade is based on team project work. Although content is most important, form will also be graded. The following input will determine the grade:

Five interim reports @ 5% each (content and form):	25%
Verbal presentation of campaigns:	20%
Final written project (content and form):	50%
Class attendance, participation in class, quiz grades, and overall attitude:	5%
Total	100%

The team project report and grade will be based on:

1. An in-depth analysis and review of the business and product situation;

2. Setting proper objectives;

3. Developing strategies that fulfill the objectives;

4. Executing strategies;

5. Developing an appropriate budget and marketing calendar;

6. Justifying all recommended actions and budgeted expenditures; and

7. Providing verbal presentation and written material in a professional manner.

Class Text: *The Successful Marketing Plan, 2/e*, Roman Hiebing and Scott Cooper

Supplementary Texts: *Advertising: From fundamentals to Strategies*, Michael L. Rothschild

The Copy Workshop/Workbook, Bruce Bendinger

CLASS SCHEDULE

Complete your due dates in the second column.

Week	Week of	Topic	Textbook Chapters
1		Introduction to Course, Business Review, Team Assignments	Introduction; Business Review (1-2)
2		Client Product Presentations and Business Review	Business Review (1-2)
3		Business Review	Business Review (1-2) Problems & Opportunities (3)
4		Business Review (Complete Business Review)	Sales Objectives (4); Target Market and Marketing Objectives (5)
5		Determining Sales Objectives; Target Market and Marketing Objectives	Positioning (6)
6		Positioning; Marketing Strategies; Communications Goals	Communications Goals (8); Advertising Message (14)
7		Advertising Objectives and Strategies (Sales Objectives, Target Market, Marketing Objectives & Strategies, Advertising Objectives & Strategies Evaluation of team members	Product/Branding/ Packaging; Pricing; Distribution; Personal Selling; Promotion (9-13)
8		Product/Branding/ Packaging; Pricing; Distribution; Personal Selling; Promotion	Media (15)
9		Media Review & Objectives (Product thru Promotion Plan)	Media (15)

Week	Week of	Topic	Textbook Chapters
10		Media Strategy, Plan and Budget/First Review of Creative	Media (15)
11		Creative Execution (<u>Media Plan and Media Budget</u>)	Merchandising; Publicity (16-17)
12		Creative Execution (*Rough Creative Executions*)	Budget, Payback Analysis, Calendar; Execution (18-19)
13		Merchandising; Publicity; Budget, Payback Analysis & Calendar; Execution	Evaluation (20)
14		In-class Presentation Rehearsals (<u>Merchandising; Publicity; Budget, Payback Analysis and Calendar</u>)	
15		Final Presentations <u>Final Written Presentation Due</u>!	In-class Student Evaluation of Instructor and Team Members

*The world of advertising and marketing is one of constant change, and so is this class schedule! Be flexible and responsive!

Two copies of the final written campaign and plans—one for the client and one for the instructor—are due no later than the date of the final presentation. Your work should be of professional caliber and should be assembled in book form. One member of each team is to act as editor on the final written presentation.

The due dates for the interim reports are listed on the class schedule. Make sure each report includes an outline of contents. The instructor will use these reports to provide feedback to the team on its progress and to raise questions for the team. Teams are encouraged to use this mechanism to its fullest by providing extensive documentation on the topic area. If used properly, the interim reports will force the team to make progress and clarify the position of each team member. <u>Historically, teams which have not taken advantage of this procedure have not done as well at the conclusion of the project.</u>

Grading of the verbal presentation to the client will be based on the content and professional nature of the presentation (what is presented verbally with use of audiovisual aids). Content will be most important in the written report. (The verbal presentation should be a summary of the written presentation.)

Scope of Final Project

Each project will include a business review, complete marketing plan, and creative executions. Justify all points as necessary and coordinate your campaign. Creative work should include:

1. At least one execution for each medium used.

2. At least one execution for each target market.

3. At least one execution for each creative strategy. (Example: concept sell execution as well as promotional execution.)

Any storyboards, ads, and merchandising materials shown in the presentation should be reduced to 8 1/2 x 11 and included in the written report.

Promotion and merchandising materials along with packaging work should have enough detail and graphics to be understood.

All work should be written by you as an <u>ad agency</u> reporting to your client.

The final written presentation should be summarized in less than 75 pages of text, but can refer to previous work on creative materials included in an appendix. There is no need to bulk the report. Remember you are writing for a busy manager. (Executional copy and visuals are not included in the 75-page limit.)

Some Random Thoughts

1. Interim reports are expected to be thorough and in professional form. The harder you work on the interim report, the easier will be the final report. Each successive interim report should build on earlier ones. Submit all prior reports along with each interim report. The business review should be fairly complete and specific when it is submitted. When writing the marketing background and plan segments, follow the style of the specific examples and formats provided in the text.

2. The guest speakers will share their real world experiences with you. Ask questions. Talk to the speakers. Use their suggestions. Ask them about job opportunities.

3. Let yourself go on creative. Be creative. Be brilliant. But, be on strategy—don't be creative for creative's sake.

4. TALK TO YOUR INSTRUCTOR IF YOU NEED HELP.

5. If you type good interim reports (on a word processor) you can possibly save some of the tables or text for the final report. Submit a copy for comments. Keep the original disk.

6. Open your ad agency and begin to function as such as soon as possible. Choose a name for your agency and act as if you are really part of that agency.

7. All campaign plans must make sense. Each component part should be coordinated. All recommendations are to be justified. The plan must be usable and viable. You will meet these criteria by the end of the semester and present a plan which will hopefully rival the work done by professional advertising agencies.

8. Be creative in your presentations to the client. But don't be hokey. Rehearse the presentation. Rehearse. And rehearse. If you turn the client off in the verbal presentation, the written presentation might not be reviewed.

Pros and Cons of the Course

Just as it is necessary to isolate the problems and opportunities of the product before preparing the marketing plan, it is necessary to beware of pros and cons in teaching this course from both the instructor and students point of view.

Pros

1. Students enjoy this application course more than the more typical class of lectures, text readings, and exams. Accordingly, they become very involved. However, this application requires extensive one-on-one involvement with the agency teams and the individual students.

2. Most students feel it is a very important course in their preparation for an advertising or marketing career and are willing to invest a considerable amount of time getting the most out of the course.

3. Because students apply their skills from previous courses, they see results and feel they really are learning—a lot!

4. Because students must translate principle into action, they learn to think for themselves and solve problems. Because this is a translation course, there is a tendency to over teach, providing students with your solutions rather than their own.

5. Each student, by having to work with other students in a team setting, has the responsibility of performing a specific function, i.e. account executive, creative director, media director, etc., and needs to positively interface with other team members in order to develop a quality, competitive campaign.

6. Students not only receive a grade but also a near-to-real-world experience with a pragmatic marketing plan document and advertising campaign that they can draw upon in their job interviews and entry-level positions.

7. The course provides students with a decision-making structure they will be able to use throughout their careers. While individual facts memorized for a multiple choice exam fade from memory, a decision-making format, such as the disciplined campaign development process detailed in the course, will be used over and over again. Once students are exposed to the process, it will be theirs to use as a basis for strategic advertising and marketing decisions.

Cons

1. Most students believe the campaigns course to be the most demanding (particularly in time required) of any course they have ever taken. Accordingly, it is necessary to make students aware, right from the start, of the demands of the course and stress that they should not take the course if they cannot devote an above-average amount of time.

   Most students believe that the time required for this course should make it worth twice the credits given. However, the instructor should continually point out that the student is taking this course primarily for the real-world learning experience—not just for credits. Further, this course can help students in obtaining an advertising or marketing job and be of major assistance in early performance in the new position.

2. Because there is much to be done and a long path to the final presentation and written document, there is a tendency for some of the student teams to fall behind and become discouraged. For this reason, it is necessary for students to begin working hard and fast from start to finish and take one step at a time, doing the best job possible with each interim report. If this is done, the final verbal and written presentations come together toward the end of the course almost magically.

3. The course never seems to let students relax, such as after a midterm exam in other courses. Students cannot afford to take it easy in the beginning weeks of the course; they must begin immediately gathering and organizing data for the business review. On the positive side, once the students begin creating the campaign during the last third of the course, most seem to get caught up in the race and catch fire.

4. Because this is an applications course and the world of advertising and marketing is not a science, there are no 100 percent right or wrong answers. Accordingly, the students become frustrated when you cannot give them a direct answer or the solution for their particular product situation. It's all in how students themselves interpret the situation and apply the action—just as in real life. In this situation, try to ask students questions that will lead them back to define the core of the problem. Have them think of products with similar problems and review the end-approach. Also point out the step-by-step decision process in the text they should follow to arrive at their own solution. Students must be reminded to be innovative when they become stymied. For example, if they cannot find some piece of data for the product to make a decision, interpolating data from a similar product might provide some insight into making a decision for their product.

5. Because different students with varied backgrounds, personalities, and talents must work closely together as a team toward a common goal, interpersonal problems can develop between team members. The most prevalent problems experienced include some member(s) of the team not carrying their fair share of the workload, and specific personality conflicts and differences of opinion as to the direction to be taken in the marketing plan and execution of the campaign. To help eliminate the inequality of team members' contribution and give due credit for individuals with experience, we have included a team member evaluation form to be completed by each student midway through the course and at the end of the course. The selection of a strong account executive to lead each student team will help but never eliminate the interpersonal team conflicts. To a certain extent, this conflict is part of the learning process.

6. Don't expect the students to retain vast amounts of information from previous courses taken in preparation for this course. Realistically, you can't assume in-depth knowledge regarding specific disciplines whether or not the corresponding course was taken for credit. Therefore, you must review each discipline with the students prior to their application of the specific discipline. For example, be prepared to go over the basics of media such as GRPs, CPM, and the strengths and weaknesses of each medium before you discuss media planning.

Course Preparation

Just as we believe that in order to have good marketing and advertising *execution*, there must first be good *preparation*, we believe preparation and having a well thought-out plan for this course is an important key to making this a successful course. Accordingly, we have listed below what we believe are key considerations in preparation for this course.

1. Decide up front what you want your students to master from this course. Specifically, a good first step is to list the objectives for the course or update your objectives if you have previously taught the course. For example, is the major emphasis to be put on preparing the advertising materials for the campaign, i.e. commercials and ads, than developing a comprehensive marketing plan along with a campaign? Or, will the course objectives call for a marketing plan requiring not just

149

sales objectives, target market, marketing objectives and strategies, and positioning, but also plan segments for distribution, pricing, publicity, etc.? Do you want to create a head-to-head competitive environment or let student teams choose their own product for which to develop a plan and campaign? Or, do you want to provide one case or project for all students, such as that included in the final section of this guide?

2. Have a thorough understanding of the course text, instructor's manual, pertinent chapters of the supplementary text, and reference materials to be used by students.

3. Prepare a comprehensive syllabus. (See the example class schedule at the beginning of the section.) The more comprehensive the syllabus, the more the students will understand the course components and what is expected of them. Accordingly, there will be less questions and wheel spinning by the students as the course progresses and they prepare the specific components of the marketing plan and campaign. With a well thought-out syllabus, students can better plan their time and meet the specific due dates with quality planning documents and communication materials.

In preparing a class schedule for a tri-semester school year, you can reduce the 15-week course to 10 weeks, adjusting the 15-week class schedule as follows:

— Eliminate one week of business review class discussion.

— Combine your discussion of advertising objectives and strategies with marketing objectives/strategies and positioning of the previous week.

— Eliminate discussion of product branding/packaging, pricing, personal selling, and promotion by answering any questions regarding the text readings during the week of media class discussion. The marketing plan segments would then be due with the media plan interim report.

— Eliminate one week of media plan class discussion.

— Limit class discussion on creative execution to one instead of two weeks.

If you feel it necessary to reduce the student work load for the 10-week course, you can also eliminate the chapter readings and preparations of marketing plan segments on pricing, distribution, personal selling, merchandising, and publicity. All other course text readings and interim reports would remain intact for the class schedule.

4. In addition to a class schedule as part of the syllabus, you might also want to prepare the following handouts (or adapt the example materials in the Appendix).

— A written notice to be distributed to students the first day of classes listing what is expected of students along with the rewards for those who complete the course.

— Student background questionnaire (career interests course taken, job experience, etc.). This is to be completed and returned to you by students the first day of class to help in formation of equitable and compatible agency teams.

— Evaluation form of agency team associates for use at the midterm and the conclusion of course to determine the quantity and quality of work by each team member.

— Client/agency evaluation form for the final presentations to be completed by client and agency practitioners reviewing the student teams' work.

5. Gather reference materials and place in library, or determine where reference resources are available on campus for students' use in preparation of their business review and marketing plan.

6. If possible, make arrangements for students with diverse academic backgrounds (such as business, journalism or arts) to work together on teams. The interaction of students with diverse academic backgrounds and skills dramatically improves both the quality of the final campaign and the real-world learning experience of the students.

7. While a campaigns course can be effectively executed for any consumer or business-to-business product and retail or service organization with national, regional, or local distribution, probably the ideal situation is an existing or new consumer goods product with national distribution. This type of product will incorporate marketing to a business-to-business trade target(s) as well as consumer target(s) and give students the opportunity to market both on a local and regional marketing basis, with the opportunity to employ all the available media.

   If you are structuring a competitive environment for students and thus need to secure the desired products for students' campaigns, you'll want to get commitments from companies to participate in the course a minimum of one month before the start of classes. As part of the commitment, ask the client to make a presentation of the product and its situation early in the course and to be available for the evaluation of students' verbal presentations the last week of class. The more background data the client can provide, the better. If possible, the client background presentation should include product history, including examples of related advertising and promotions materials, sales and profit history and expectations, product costs that make up the client's selling price and the competitive situation from the client's perspective. The client should also be available throughout the duration of the course for student questions screened by and asked through the instructor to avoid duplication in questions and the inefficient use of the client's time.

8. In order to give students a realistic perspective of the current marketing environment and provide input for the development of a marketing plan and campaign, attempt to schedule guest lectures from the various disciplines at the appropriate times through the duration of the course. These same guest lectures will then, with your client, become the Plans Board that will evaluate the student campaigns at the conclusion of the course. In addition to inviting the client(s) to the class presentation, other practitioners that might guest lecture, include an account executive, researcher, creative director, copy writer, art director, and media director/planner.

9. Secure a classroom that is conducive to both lectures and for students to work in groups so that agency teams can prepare their plans and executional materials. Ideally, a classroom on one level with tables and chairs that can be moved to facilitate individual student work groups is ideal.

10. Reserve a presentation room during last week of course for student team stand-up presentations. It should have ample room for all students and outside evaluators and be equipped with the necessary audiovisual equipment.

Course Commencement (First Two Weeks)

We believe the first and last two weeks of this campaign are by far the most demanding for the instructor. Accordingly we will discuss in detail the instructor's and students' task for each of these two week periods—the first two-week period under course commencement and the last two-week period at the end of this course discussion under course resolution.

In the discussion of the first two weeks of classes, we assume the class will meet two times per week. However, the material can also be adapted for three class sessions per week.

First Class Session

1. Make sure you have only qualified students enrolled in the course.

2. Provide an overview in the course by taking students through the syllabus, answering student questions while strongly suggesting that each student thoroughly read the syllabus before the next class and bring any questions they may have regarding the syllabus and course to next class.

3. In addition to distributing the syllabus, hand out a written notice (example included in the Appendix) that details what is required of each student and what they can expect in return. The intent is to make students aware of the demands of the course while encouraging those who do not have adequate time available or a sincere interest in real-world advertising and marketing applications to *drop* the course. Students without the time or desire will not enjoy or genuinely learn while putting unfair workload burdens on other students in their agency team and limiting other students from taking this course.

    Distribute the Evaluation of Agency Associates form at this time to reinforce the importance of full student participation with each team.

4. Although not critical, distribute a copy f the evaluation form. This form will be completed by a grading team of advertising and marketing practitioners after each team makes their final presentation during the last week of class. This reinforces the fact that real-world practitioners, from outside the class, will be personally evaluating their work and solely responsible for giving 20% of the student's grade.

5. Announce the clients and corresponding products for which the agency teams (once formed) will be competing. Also specify which class days each client will be making their respective presentations. If you are not structuring a competition for the student teams, make it clear that once each agency is formed, students within each team will be responsible for product selection and notifying the instructor of their own product no later than the end of the second week of classes.

6. Make it clear that each student will be assigned to an agency team and will take on a specific responsibility. For example, each team usually includes:

Account Executive	Creative Director
Art Director	Media Director
Promotions Director	Research Director

    All students within each team should be involved in all aspects of the planning and campaign execution. However, each student, based on the person's respective agency position, would be primarily responsible for coordinating the task associated with that agency position. The agency positions will vary dependent on the tasks to be accomplished and student interest and skills. Once the agency teams are formed, team members will decide which position will be assigned to each student.

7. Usually more than one individual within teach team has an interest in becoming the account executive. It should be pointed out that the account executive usually experiences the most frustration in helping to motivate and enhance the working relationship of the individual team members. Further, it is the account executive's responsibility not only to provide team leadership but make sure the specific due dates are met. Meeting the due dates for the interim reports along with the organization and delivery of the final verbal presentation and the written document are the account executives' ultimate responsibilities. The account executive can usually anticipate contributing the *most time* of all the marketing team members. it is necessary for the account executive to provide the necessary leadership, therefore the account executive should read ahead in the text and have read the entire text within the first four weeks of the course.

8. The other team members are required to read weekly assigned chapters in the text plus, within the first few weeks, read ahead and have an understanding of those chapters that pertain to their specific individual agency team responsibility.

9. Review the key elements in the introduction of the text with students. It is especially important to review the definition of marketing, marketing plan, and disciplined marketing planning because it becomes the foundation for the development of the product campaigns. Make sure students read the introductory chapter before the next class period so that you can quiz them on the subject of marketing planning and they can ask intelligent questions regarding the subject.

10. Distribute, and receive back after the first class, the completed student questionnaires. Then, before the next class period, review each completed student questionnaire and organize student teams based on students' previous academic course work, job experience, non job-related group activities and career aspirations. In forming agency teams attempt to be as equitable as possible in order to arrive at teams with individuals representing similar backgrounds.

11. Because the account executive position is so important to a team, you might want to interview those students interested in this position after class. If possible, question these students regarding previous classes taken, related internships, grades received, overall grade point, group leadership positions, time availability, and their understanding of the commitment necessary to be a successful agency team account executive.

Second Class Session

1. Announce the individual team members for each agency and the *recommendations* for each account executive position. We believe the individual student teams should make the final decision on who is to be the account executive as well as the other agency team positions. It's best that the teams start making their own decisions as soon as possible. (However, we find the teams usually take our suggestions for account executives and are the better for it.)

2. Give each team a number for descriptive purposes. Assign group areas within the classroom and have the respective team members take their seats within the designated group area within the classroom. From that time forward, team members sit in their designated areas for the remainder of the course. With this type of seating arrangement students see themselves as an integrated agency team and are in a position to work together when they are in class.

3. When employing a competitive class environment, once the groups are formed, assign three agency teams (Groups 1, 2, and 3) one product and the three remaining teams (Groups 4, 5, and 6) another product. Each team then is required for their next class session to select an agency team name and decide on individual responsibilities within the team. Each team will submit to the instructor in writing for the next class session the name of the agency team along with each student team member's name and their corresponding agency position.

4. Review what goes into a business review or situation analysis outline. (An outline description is included under business review in manual.) Each team is to submit to the instructor an outline no later than the end of the second week of classes so that each team will effectively and correctly have a road map to follow in gathering and organizing the background data. Based on what is included in each outline, you can suggest any additions and revisions needed in preparation of this business review data. While the business review outline is being prepared, individual team members should begin to search out business sources and gather data for their specific product.

5. Because the art students are not usually as quantitatively oriented as the other students, it is suggested that they be the agency team member responsible for gathering and reviewing their product's category advertising, packaging, and merchandising materials.

6. It also is a good idea to suggest that the students review the previous year's final campaign report(s) (if available) that would have been placed on reserve in the library. This gives the students an approximation of what their final work will entail and give them something to "shoot for and beat" in terms of quality and quantity.

Second Week of Classes

During the second week of class, students are ready to hear the in-class client presentations (if you have obtained actual clients for the class). We require the attendance of all students at client presentations. This allows them to gain exposure to different client personalities, types of data, methods of marketing, and new ideas.

Course Maintenance

Overall Course Mechanics

1. Make every effort to have students stay current with the weekly text readings. Pursuant to the example syllabus, students should have read assigned chapters by the specified class week so that they have an overall understanding of what is discussed in class. The instructor can then effectively use class time to highlight key elements of the chapter and to answer any pertinent student questions. In their evaluation of the course, many students have requested that the instructor not review what was in the text but discuss new and related material regarding the class topic. Accordingly in the portions of this manual discussing how to use the text, we have included additional meaningful discussion topics. However, we have found in the majority of instances that many students have not read and/or thoroughly understand the methodology included in the text. For this reason, make sure students understand the basics of the text before interjecting more involved issues.

2. To help keep students current in their understanding of the text material and to make the class discussions interesting as possible you can:

   — Ask students questions regarding the key methods and principles included in the text. The "Dos and Don'ts" at the end of each chapter are an effective tool to use in asking questions.

   — Have students provide examples they have observed or experienced which relate to the methods and principles provided in the test.

   — To help insure mainstream students have an overall understanding of the specific "how to methodology," it is effective to make overhead transparencies of selected pages from the text and lead the class discussion from the overheads.

   — Get as much in-class student participation as possible continually throughout the course.

3. Students generally enjoy guest lectures. If possible, schedule practitioners with varied positions from both the agency and advertising side of the business. Have them discuss what the responsibilities of their positions, problems and opportunities encountered in their work, their approach to meeting these challenges, and how they work through related issues similar to what the students in the class are facing. Accordingly, schedule the guest lectures relative to the student tasks to be completed. For example, we schedule an agency account executive early in the course to discuss how to lead and coordinate the marketing planning and campaign development as well as how to interface with the client. Likewise we bring in a researcher during the business review process to discuss the assembling and evaluation of data.

Ask guest lecturers to bring along examples of their work whether it be quantitative, such as for a media discussion, or qualitative, for creative discussions. For creative discussion, we ask both the copywriter and art director to bring to class not only the finished broadcast and print materials but the storyboards or layouts and creative strategies from which the finished advertising was developed. Presenting all these examples (strategy to finished materials) helps the students see the whole process of creative development as they begin their creative development.

Interaction Between Instructor and Students

Because this course is one of application, it is imperative that the instructor maintain on-going personal contact with the students to explain methods, ask and answer questions, provide examples relative to the students specific and current challenges, provide encouragement, and point out consequences for specific action or inaction in dealing with specific issues. It is important that the instructor meet with the *student teams* on a regular basis (weekly if possible) either before, during, or after class. There is a continual need to answer questions and check the progress of the team's work. Provide directional guidance, but don't provide the student's strategic direction. Force them to work through the "how to" process on their own.

Meet with Account Executives and Art Directors

Because the account executive is very important to each team's success, it is worthwhile for the instructor to meet with each account executive individually or as a group to discuss their methods of leading and coordinating the overall team effort. It is usually productive to meet with the team account executives as a group at approximately five weeks and then ten weeks into the course. You will find many of the problems and questions raised by the account executives are very common to all of them and can be dealt with accordingly.

Because art students' academic background and skills are often dissimilar to both journalism and business students, many arts students seem somewhat displaced and confused early in the course. For this reason it is helpful for the instructor to meet with the art students as a group two weeks and seven weeks into the course to answer questions and specifically outline their responsibilities and how they can more fully contribute to the team assignments. This is particularly true early on in the course during the more quantitative business review process.. Usually, being more qualitative in nature, art students seem most comfortable gathering and reviewing the category's advertising, packaging, promotional and merchandising materials from both a communication and design basis. At the seven-week meeting, the creative conceptual and executional process should be reviewed. Discuss what is expected of the art students and explain how they should proceed in this process. If at all possible, try to have their art students' professor present at these meetings to help facilitate relevant discussion and help bridge the gap from their background to the tasks of this course. The art professor should also be invited to attend the final stand-up presentations to see the final work of the art students presented and critiqued.

Interim Reports

The interim reports are building blocks in the step-by-step process of preparing the finalized marketing plan and campaign. The better the work done for the interim reports, the better the final stand-up and written presentations.

Each interim report should include an up-front outline of contents and be professional in appearance, submitted on time, with no exceptions. After the student teams review the instructor's written comments of the interim reports, the teams should meet with the instructor to have their questions answered and to determine how they can improve the work submitted. Based on the instructor's comments, the interim reports should be revised by the student teams and resubmitted with the next interim report. The more work put into the interim reports, the easier the preparation of the final stand-up and written presentations.

The most difficult interim report is usually the business review because it is the first. Students are generally unfamiliar with the planning process, and underestimate the time needed to properly prepare this portion of the campaign. Students tend to procrastinate early in the course. For these reasons, it is important to impress upon the student teams the need to organize immediately and begin work on the marketing background segment of the campaign. Putting together an effective business review outline within the first two weeks of the course is an important part of this up-front preparation.

Discourage students from attempting to do their own primary research as part of the business review process because of the time and experience required to generate usable primary data. Encourage them to informally talk with consumers to develop a qualitative feel for the product and its users.

Peer Evaluation

The evaluation of fellow team associates midway through the course is critical to determine those students who are contributing their fair share to the team effort and those students who are not. You should impress upon the students the need for honest peer evaluation and that their peer evaluation will be kept confidential. You can be assured that if the same team member is rated poorly by a number of fellow team students, there is real problem of fair contribution by this member. Art students usually score lower in this midterm evaluation because their qualitative background and skills do not let them contribute as much to the business review process for their team. Art students usually always contribute considerably more the second half of the course when they begin to become involved in the creative process and the visual execution of all the campaign materials.

After reviewing the individual evaluations, meet with the low-level contributors individually or as a group to listen to their point of view and to remind them of the course commitments they made the first week of class. You might also point out the consequences in store for them (lower grade, your increased personal attention of them in class, etc.) unless they become self-motivated to do their fair share of the overall team effort.

Creative Development

Because creative development is so important to the course and takes a considerable amount of time, we deviate from the discipline planning process in the text by moving the advertising planning process up to the seventh week of the course. Advertising objectives and strategies can thus be prepared and the executional process of preparing the campaign materials can begin with enough time for adequate preparation. It is important that the creative director and art director initiate this process early enough and simultaneous to the preparation of the other elements of the campaign. While the creative director and art director are prime movers of the creative process, all team members should be involved in brainstorming ideas and creative development of the materials. Once the creative process begins, it is beneficial to meet weekly with the creative director and art director to see their work, answer questions, and provide them with an outside point of view of their creative work.

Course Resolution (Last Two Weeks of Class)

The last two weeks of the campaigns course are extremely busy for both the instructor and students. The following activities take place:

— Preparation of the final campaign report, including the written marketing plan and creative materials.

— Rehearsal of the stand-up presentation by the student teams.

— Stand-up student team presentations before evaluating practitioners.

— Final in-class peer evaluation.

— Instructor's review of teams' written presentation.

— Instructor's review of the client or agency practitioner evaluation forms.

— Student final evaluations of fellow agency associates.

— Calculation of final grade.

Preparing of Final Campaign Report

The vast majority of the final report for each group should be completed by second to last week of class. If the student teams prepared quality interim marketing reports an revised the reports based upon the instructor's comments, as well as continually worked on the creative development of the campaign materials, this should not be a problem. Although the final budgets and calendar are sill being finalized along with creative materials, the written marketing plan should be complete. The written document should indicate both the marketing background and plan portions presented in an order similar to that recommended by the disciplined marketing planning methodology of the text. Pursuant to the example syllabus, the final report should limit the marketing plan to seventy-five pages, with reference materials and copies of creative materials included in the Appendix of the document. Two copies of the typed report should be prepared for the course—one for the instructor and one for the client—both submitted when the stand-up presentation is given. Students will also want to make copies of the final campaign report for each of the team members.

The creative director, art director, and remaining team members should have been diligently working on creative development since the positioning and creative strategy were submitted the seventh week of class. Therefore all potential creative campaign examples (commercials, ads, brochures, packaging, merchandising pieces, press releases, premiums, etc.) should be in a near final stage by the second last week of class.

Before they finalize the campaign report, have student teams once again review the example campaign reports from previous classes (if available) to help them with the format and creative portion of the presentations.

Rehearsal for Stand-Up Presentation

Although holding a rehearsal for each of the teams is very time consuming, it is worthwhile for the following reasons:

— It motivates student teams to prepare, earlier than normal, their marketing plan and creative campaign materials.

— Each student personally experiences presenting in front of a group and speaking prior to the final presentation.

— Each team will see what changes need to be made in their presentation technique and audiovisual materials. Does the audience understand what the team is attempting to communicate?

— Each team will get feedback on their marketing plan and campaign materials. Does the plan make sense? Are there major voids? Do the creative materials communicate? Are they attention-getting?

— After going through this "live" critique process, the students realize which changes to the plan, campaign materials, and physical presentation itself must be made and are in a position of having one week to make the necessary revisions.

The rehearsals are held over three class sessions (two noncompeting agency teams per rehearsal) the week before the presentations. For the rehearsal, each student team has 45 minutes to present its plan and campaign materials. Then each member of the reviewing team gives a critique of the presentation team. Following their critiques the instructor summarizes, adding any additional comments. The rehearsal process is involved and time consuming—it takes approximately three hours (sometimes considerably longer) for the presentation and critique by two agency teams.

For the rehearsal presentation, student teams are expected to summarize the written marketing plan using prepared overhead transparencies and other prepared audiovisual devices. Although campaign materials such as storyboards and layouts are expected to be totally finished (including color where appropriate) for the final stand-up presentation, they should be in a near final stage for rehearsal presentation and critique. The more student teams push to have their plan and campaign materials finalized for the rehearsal, the more time they have to revise their work and practice their delivery for the final stand-up presentation. Make sure student teams are aware they must practice their delivery of the presentation prior to the rehearsal in order to come across as professionals and keep their delivery within the 45-minute time period.

Presentation Mechanics (Lecture Outline)

Prior to the rehearsal, it is worthwhile for the instructor to review with the students what goes into a quality, final stand-up presentation.

1. Make sure each student team knows the target market for the presentation—the client and agency practitioners. Students need to know who they are, where they work, their positions, etc.

2. Someone from each student team should check out the room where the presentation is to be held—size of room and seating arrangement, lighting, outlets, screen placement, equipment availability, etc.

3. Make sure the visuals for the screen (charts if used) are easy to read. Also make sure students remember to:

   — Use oversized type in bold lettering.

   — Use simple concise statements in bullet not paragraph form.

   — Have fewer key points (bullets) rather than more.

   — Not talk too long without a reinforcing visual.

   — Limit the key points to each overhead to five or less (use key points as visual set-up then elaborate verbally).

   — Make sure the oral presentation and visuals coincide and reinforce each other. Don't point to a key visual and talk about something else.

   — Use a pointer or pen as a directional tool with the overheads and screen so that the audience can follow what is being presented.

4. Make sure the students present with intensity, enthusiasm, and confidence (without being cocky), always projecting a professional image. Encourage them to be personal and stand close to the

evaluators when not using the screen or presenting examples of their work, i.e., storyboards, ads, packaging, etc.

5. Make sure their presentation is ordered and well organized. Remind students to:

— Announce and visually highlight the name of the agency with the account executive introducing the individual team members.

— Provide an introduction of the presentation in terms of an outline of what is to be covered. (Tell them what you are going to tell them.)

— Deliver the body of the presentation. Present the plan with campaign materials interspersed throughout for clarification and for keeping the audience's attention and interest. (Tell them.)

— Provide a brief summary. (Tell them what you told them.)

— Ask for any questions or comments from the evaluation board.

6. The stand-up presentation should only summarize the final written campaign report. Depending on time and what is presented, various sections of the plan will be only highlighted or maybe eliminated from the stand-up presentation. Rationales should be presented for all key points made but should be presented in as brief a manner as possible.

7. Think about where your plan is vulnerable and be prepared to answer questions of the evaluators. The more questions you can think of beforehand, the better you can address them in your presentation or when the questions are asked. The better student team members respond to the evaluation questions, the better they will score on the overall evaluation.

Final Presentation

This is it! All the researching, number crunching, strategizing, agreeing and disagreeing; writing, rewriting, creating, and revising; all the late night hour meetings, rehearsing, and rehearsing, all the work—it all comes down to when the stand-up presentation is given and a final written campaign report is submitted to the client and the course instructor.

The Team Competitive Presentation Format

The three agency teams competing for the same product present their plan and campaign to the client and agency evaluators in head-to-head competition. One team after the other has forty-five minutes of presentation time after which an additional fifteen minutes is allocated for the evaluators to ask questions as well as comment and critique each team's presentation.

Presentation Evaluation

An example of an evaluation form to be used by the client and agency practitioners is included in the Appendix.

In addition to having each evaluator score each team on various components of the campaign, via the evaluation form, each practitioner is asked to provide an overall ranking of the teams. This adds to the competitive framework of the course and provides an added assistance when the instructor tallies the evaluation form and provides a grade for the stand-up presentation for each team.

Once the final course grade is calculated for each student and if there is student interest in the practitioners' evaluation and written comments, the instructor might want to copy the evaluation forms for the respective agency teams. This is another good learning tool for all students.

Elements of the Presentation

1. Students are expected to dress in appropriate business attire.

2. Overhead transparencies are recommended as the primary visual presentation tool because they are relatively simple to prepare and are relatively inexpensive. However, there might be specific elements (such as the marketing calendar) of the presentation that agency teams want to highlight with charts and/or slides.

3. In terms of the campaign's creative executional requirements, we suggest you refer to the requirements listed in the example syllabus. For the television presentation, storyboards with written copy captions are suggested *over* slides with a sound tract because storyboards are easier for students to prepare and are more reflective of how television commercials are actually presented to clients by agencies. Radio scripts can be simply read or prerecorded with music. In terms of music for television and radio commercials, the presenter can either describe or play an example of the type of music to be used. Occasionally some student teams play instruments or sing their own songs. For packaging and merchandising materials, illustrations or actual mock-up examples of the materials can be presented. All layouts of the printed materials should be presented and enough copy read (headline and lead-in copy) for evaluators to understand the message.

Final peer Evaluation

The last class session should include the final team member evaluations of each other. Also, ask students to evaluate the course and the instructor, providing their suggestions for improving the course.

Final Grade Preparation

Once the instructor has graded the written campaign report and arrived at a grade for the stand-up presentation, and after tallying the score for each team based on the practitioners' evaluations, the instructor can arrive at a composite grade. This is accomplished by combining, on a percentage basis, the average team grade of the five interim reports along with the team grades of the final written campaign report and the stand-up presentation for a final team grade. Then, along with the two agency-associate peer evaluations and the other factors of class attendance, class participation, quiz grades (if applicable) and each student's attitude, the instructor can adjust the agency team grade to arrive at a final grade for each individual student. While the individual grade is important, the real worth of this course is the applied experience students acquire as they cross the bridge from academic life to the real world of advertising and marketing.

Important Notice to All Students

You have registered for this course. Are you sure this course is right for you? Please consider the following:

1. You must be willing to work hard to balance the efforts of your project teammates.

2. You must be willing to stick out the course and not drop out midstream because a team that is short a person will suffer undue hardship.

3. Since enrollment is very limited, your presence will keep someone else from taking the course.

In return for these obligations you will receive the opportunity to develop a marketing plan along with an advertising and promotional campaign in a real world setting. The near unanimous feeling of past students has been that this course is:

1. One of the most demanding they have ever taken, requiring more work and time than any other course.

2. One of the most rewarding they have ever taken (you learn much and it's very important in preparation for a career in marketing and advertising).

3. The catalyst for a valuable campaign piece for their portfolios.

Client/Agency Practitioner Evaluations of Presentations

Team: Evaluator:

Please evaluate the team on each of the following attributes, using the 100-point scale and giving any relevant comments.

PROFESSIONAL PRESENTATION; SALESMANSHIP

0   10   20   30   40   50   60   70   80   90   100

Comments:

JUSTIFICATION OF PLAN; RATIONALE

0   10   20   30   40   50   60   70   80   90   100

Comments:

PRACTICALITY; USABILITY; SENSIBILITY

0   10   20   30   40   50   60   70   80   90   100

Comments:

COORDINATION; INTEGRATION OF PLAN AND CAMPAIGN ELEMENTS; CAMPAIGN CALENDAR

0   10   20   30   40   50   60   70   80   90   100

Comments:

SALES GOALS; TARGET MARKETS; MARKETING OBJECTIVES/STRATEGIES; POSITIONING, BRANDING

0   10   20   30   40   50   60   70   80   90   100

Comments:

CREATIVE; ADVERTISING OBJECTIVES/STRATEGIES; EXECUTION

0   10   20   30   40   50   60   70   80   90   100

Comments:

MEDIA PLAN

0   10   20   30   40   50   60   70   80   90   100

Comments:

NONADVERTISING—PROMOTION; MERCHANDISING; PUBLICITY

0   10   20   30   40   50   60   70   80   90   100

Comments:

BUDGET/PAYOUT

0   10   20   30   40   50   60   70   80   90   100

Comments:

PLEASE MAKE ADDITIONAL COMMENTS ON A SEPARATE SHEET

Evaluation of Agency Associates

Given 100 points, assign points to yourself and your teammates based on the QUANTITY of work done by each member. (Ex: If all members contributed equally in amount of work done, you would give 16.7 points to each member of a six-person team or 20 points to each member for a five-person team. If a person did more or less work, you should assign more or less points to that person.)

Name   Points

Now evaluate each member of the team based on the *quality* of work done by that person. That is, how good was each person's contribution? Again, divide 100 points among yourself and your teammates.

Name   Points

Any comments or amplifications would be useful, helpful, and appreciated.

Evaluator's name:

Thank you

Background Questionnaire

1. Name

2. Degree (working for) and major:

    Degree:
    Major:
    Minor:

3. Year in School (Jr., Sr., Grad., etc.):

4. Have you had:

	Yes	No	Now Taking	Instructor
A. Principles of Advertising				
B. Advertising Copy & Layout				
C. Advanced Copy & Layout				
D. Advertising Media				
E. Introduction to Survey Research				
F. Communication Research Methods				
G. Introductory Marketing				
H. Marketing Research				
I. Marketing Communications				
J. Promotional Strategies				

5. List the psychology, sociology, and consumer behavior courses you have had and the instructor in each.

6. Briefly describe any advertising experience you have had including prior student projects.

7.   Do you feel you have any ability as an artist (enough to do rough layouts, renderings, etc.)?

     Yes   No   Don't Know

8.   What is your career goal? (What do you expect to be doing 10 years from now?)

9.   What has been your work experience over the past five years?

10. What organized non job activities have you participated in over the past five years? Did you hold a specific position in any of those organizations?

11. Do you want to be a team account executive in this class?

     Yes   No

12. Why do you feel you should be an account executive?

13. What is/are your phone number(s)? When can you generally be reached?

NOTES

NOTES